This is an excellent guide to spiritual life and growth. . . . Jim Harnish has a handle on the unique challenges men face, and he writes about them with grace and strength. Read it and grow!

—John Ortberg, author and pastor
Willow Creek Community Church,
South Barrington, Illinois

Men and women will find good news and encouragement in *Passion, Power & Praise.*

—Bishop Charlene P. Kammerer

Sensitive yet straightforward . . . stimulating, challenging, and helpful. Every man will see himself not only as he is, but, more importantly, as God intended. . . . A real contribution to the field of spiritual formation.

—Bishop Woodie White

I have two sons and four grandsons. I will give this book to each and believe that if they read it they will be better men because they will better understand themselves and the two great mysteries we call life and God.

—Bishop Rueben P. Job

Passion, Power & Praise is a must-read. . . . I can never thank Jim enough for its contribution to my own life.

—Dick Wills, Senior Pastor
Christ United Methodist Church,
Fort Lauderdale, Florida

Passion, Power& Praise

A Model for Men's Spirituality from the Life of David

James A. Harnish

Abingdon Press
Nashville

PASSION, POWER, AND PRAISE:
A Model for Men's Spirituality from the Life of David

Copyright © 2000 by Abingdon Press

This book is printed on acid-free paper.

Library of Congress Cataloging-in-Publication Data

Harnish, James A.
    Passion, power & praise: a model for men's spirituality from the life of David / James A. Harnish
        p. cm.
    ISBN 0-687-03630-5
    1. Christian men—Religious life. 2. David, King of Israel. I. Title: Passion, power, and praise. II. Title.

BV4528.2 .H35 2000
248.8'42—dc21

                                                                    00-038610

Scripture quotations, unless otherwise indicated, are from the *New Revised Standard Version of the Bible,* copyright 1989, Division of Christian Education of the National Council of the Churches of Christ in the United States of America. Used by permission. All rights reserved.

Scripture quotations noted JBP are from *The New Testament in Modern English,* Revised Edition, by J. B. Phillips, published by Macmillan Publishing Co. Copyright © J. B. Phillips, 1958, 1959, 1960, 1972.

Scripture quotations noted KJV are from the King James Version of the Bible.

Scripture quotations noted The Message are from *The Message.* Copyright © Eugene H. Peterson, 1993, 1994, 1995. Used by permission of NavPress Publishing Group.

Scripture quotations noted NIV are taken from the *Holy Bible: New International Version®.* NIV®. Copyright © 1973, 1978, 1984 by the International Bible Society. Used by permission of Zondervan Publishing House. All rights reserved.

Scripture quotations noted TEV are from the *Today's English Version*—Second Edition. Copyright © 1992 by American Bible Society. Used by permission.

The quotation on page 39 is from a prayer by Anselm translated in *The English Spirit: The Little Gidding Anthology of English Spirituality*, published in 1987 by Darton, Longman and Todd.

The quotation of song lyrics on page 138 is from "Something Beautiful," words by Gloria Gaither, music by William J. Gaither. Copyright © 1971 William J. Gaither, Inc. ASCAP. All rights controlled by Gaither Copyright Management. Used by permission.

Quotations on pages 46 and 48 from "Nonviolence and Racial Justice" by Martin Luther King, Jr., are copyright 1957 by Martin Luther King, Jr., copyright renewed 1985 by Coretta Scott King.

Quotations from *Markings* by Dag Hammarskjöld, trans. Auden/Sjoberg, are made on pages 15, 17, 76, and 131. Translation copyright © 1964 by Alfred A. Knopf, Inc. and Faber & Faber Ltd. Reprinted by permission of Alfred A. Knopf, a Division of Random House Inc.

00 01 02 03 04 05 06 07 08 09—10 9 8 7 6 5 4 3 2 1

MANUFACTURED IN THE UNITED STATES OF AMERICA

For

"Brothers, for whom I am in the pain of childbirth,

until Christ is formed in you"

Galatians 4:19, adapted

"A spiritual life is simply a life in which all that we do comes from the center, where we are anchored in God: a life soaked through and through by a sense of His reality and claim, and self-given to the great movement of His will."

Evelyn Underhill, *Communion, Community, Commonweal: Readings for Spiritual Leadership*

Contents

Acknowledgments

I know how David felt when he wrote, "The lines have fallen for me in pleasant places" (Psalm 16:6, adapted). As a pastor under a bishop's appointment, I've been as fortunate as the guy who was playing tuba the day it rained silver dollars! The people in the congregations I have been appointed to serve have helped me become a healthier, happier man than I ever could have become on my own. I shout the gratitude of the psalmist: "How excellent are the Lord's faithful people! / My greatest pleasure is to be with them" (Psalm 16:3 TEV). This book grew directly out of my life with the Lord's faithful people at Trinity United Methodist Church, DeLand, Florida; Howe Memorial United Methodist Church, Crescent City, Florida; St. Luke's United Methodist Church at Windermere, Orlando, Florida; and Hyde Park United Methodist Church, Tampa, Florida. My interest in masculine spirituality resulted from listening to men in small groups, retreats, counseling sessions, downtown lunches, parking-lot debates, letters, and e-mail messages both in and outside the church. For each of these relationships I am profoundly grateful.

The men and women who have taught me to live from the inside out are too many to name, but I must express gratitude for Peter Ferrara, who encouraged this project from the very beginning, and for Chris Crotty, Jane Brownlee, Neil James, Steve Singleton, Glenn Jackson, and Bruce Tigert, who served as the "test market" for this book and helped improve it. My spiritual growth has been nurtured by friendships with fellow pastors, including Dick Wills, Phil Roughton, Terri Hill, Bernie Lieving, LeeAnn Inman, and the "clergy cronies" retreat group: Bob Bushong, Wayne Curry, John Hill, Jeff Stiggins, Rob Parsons, Tim Smiley, Gary Spencer, and Dan Johnson. Hyde Park United Methodist Church granted the sabbatical, and Glenn and Ginger Jackson provided the Great Smoky Mountains retreat where the first draft was completed. My wife, Marsha, has helped shape this book in more ways than she realizes. Like the psalmist, "I'm happy from the inside out, and from the outside in, I'm firmly formed" (Psalm 16:9 *The Message*).

Now, where did I put my tuba?

—James A. Harnish

Farewell to the Lone Ranger

This book is for men and for the women who love them. It is for men who search for a deeper, richer, more passionate manhood and for women who long for them to find it. It is for real men who wrestle with the often-conflicting realities of success and failure, sex and power, friendship and fear. It is for that growing number of men who are now as serious about getting in touch with their souls as they once were about getting ahead, getting a woman, and getting rich. Having gotten most of what they wanted, they are now concerned about getting what they really need, getting old, and getting ready to die. This book is for ordinary men who, in the ordinary passages of masculine experience, search for an extraordinary relationship with God that will unite their human powers into an exuberant expression of praise. It is for men who want to explore the ways in which the purpose of God is being worked out in the rough-and-tumble journey of their lives. And it is for women who long to feel the passion, understand the power, and share a song of praise with the men they love.

In the years that have passed since I started to shave, discovered sex, and got my driver's license, we have experienced a seismic shift in our understanding of male identity. I am a vintage baby boomer—born in 1947, high school class of '65—which means that some very clearly defined images of manhood were imprinted on the TV screen in my preadolescent brain.

Every Saturday morning, my brother and I watched the Lone Ranger ride across the range with Tonto, his faithful and subservient companion, at his side. The Lone Ranger was dressed in white, though back then I never questioned how he managed to keep that outfit so clean! His enigmatic identity was hidden by a black mask, so that every episode ended with the same haunting question: "Who *was* that masked man?" He was the "White Knight" of the TV Western, the defender of the poor and helpless, the upholder of all things good, the relationally detached and emotionally dispassionate savior of frail and helpless weaklings who suffered injustice in a heartless world.

On Saturday night, Mom and Dad joined us around the old Sylvania for *Gunsmoke,* which opened with a bold camera shot through the A-framed legs of Matt Dillon as he whipped out his weapon and blew away an anonymous bad guy. With the same imperturbable presence as the Lone Ranger, Marshal Dillon would saunter over for a drink with the invincible Miss Kitty. The exact nature of their relationship was left undefined, as were the details of her profession and the precise nature of the business transactions that were carried out on the second floor of her saloon. It never occurred to me that there might be some moral inconsistency between the heroes I watched on Saturday and the stories I heard in Sunday school the next morning. In both places, the male roles were as clear as the desert sun.

When I looked for TV archetypes of my contemporary world, I flipped the channel to the Cleavers and *Leave It to Beaver.* They were the perfectly polished mirror image of the white, middle-class, nuclear family culture in which I lived. There were, of course, a few differences. Their house was much larger, neater, and better furnished than ours. Ward made a lot more money than my father, but he seemed to hang around home a lot more than my dad did, too. (Does anyone know what Ward actually *did* for a living?) In contrast to June, my mother never wore earrings or a pearl necklace in the kitchen. I remember June with a worried look on her face and a tremulous anxiety in her voice as she pleaded with her all-knowing, all-protecting husband, "Ward, do something!" Go get 'em, Ward! The suburban cowboy-savior comes to the rescue!

If I tired of Eddie Haskell kissing up to the Cleavers, I could change channels to check in on *Father Knows Best,* where Robert Young portrayed the archetype of the perfect father. Jim Anderson was a lot like Ward, except that in addition to his son, appropriately named Bud, he had to deal with two daughters whom he called Princess and Kitten, a fact that sometimes complicated his life but never abrogated his inherent ability to resolve every family crisis. My memory is that he went to work even less than Ward Cleaver, though he was no match for Ozzie Nelson, who never seemed to go to work at all! (Ironically, Robert Young died while I was completing this book. We learned that the actor, whose life was so perfect on television, had suffered from alcoholism and depression in real life. *The San Francisco Chronicle* quoted him asking, "What gave you the idea [the show] was real?" [*The San Francisco Chronicle*, 28 July 1998, p. A19]).

It is an understatement to say we've come a long way, baby! It is a gigantic shift from the Lone Ranger and Tonto to *NYPD Blue*. It's a long and winding road from Matt Dillon through Alan Alda to Jerry Seinfeld. More than a picket fence separates June Cleaver and Ally McBeal. And the distance between the male role models on *Father Knows Best* and *Everybody Loves Raymond* can only be measured in light years.

As a result of the changing cultural images of manhood, many of us are searching for new ways to understand ourselves and our relationships with others. "New-age" wild men beat drums in the forest; Christian "PromiseKeepers" pack stadiums and shout cheers for Jesus; African American men march on Washington; corporate CEOs try to define the boundaries of sexual harassment; white-male-backlash politicians decry affirmative action; and a whole lot of ordinary guys who may never express their search openly are trying to get in touch with their guts and with one another in ways that will enable them to grow into the fullness of life that they deeply desire but have not yet found.

In one of my favorite books from the "men's movement," *Fire in the Belly*, Sam Keen called for "a new vision of manhood—a vision of man with fire in his belly and passion in his heart" (New York: Bantam, 1991, p. 7). He shared his growth experiences in a group of men he called "The Society for the Protection and Encouragement of Righteous Manhood," or "SPERM." My attempt in this book is to put another spin on the shaping of that "new vision of manhood" by looking at male spirituality through the story of one particular man named David, the hero-king of biblical history who ruled over Israel and Judah one thousand years before the birth of Christ.

These days, political "spin doctors" would clean up David's image by hiding the more sordid details of his life. That may, in fact, be what the writers of the Old Testament Book of Chronicles attempted to do. By contrast, the books of First and Second Samuel are ruthlessly honest in their description of a man who, for all his greatness, was also one of the most tragically flawed and genuinely human characters in the Bible.

David was chosen by God in childhood, victorious over Goliath in adolescence, eloquent in his poetry, passionate in his friendship, magnificent in his grief, courageous with his armies, astute with his political instincts, and faithful in his death. He was also manipulative with his royal power, self-destructive in his sexual desires, blindly irresponsible as a parent, inconsistent in his obedience to God, and impotent at the end. In the triumph and tragedy of his story, we can see many of the very real human struggles we continue to face today, but we also see the amazing faithfulness and redemptive purpose of God being worked out in often inscrutable ways in his life.

This book describes a vision of male spirituality that is modeled by God's relationship with David and is fulfilled in Jesus of Nazareth, often called "the son of David." I am convinced that we will not find the meaning of our manhood by thumbing through the pages of *TV Guide,* by scanning the "men's" magazines in the airport bookstore, or by poking around in the narrow confines of our own subjective spiritual experience. We will find our "new vision of manhood" by discovering the creative purpose and redemptive action of God that is revealed in the story of God's covenant relationship with humanity in the Scriptures and made flesh in Jesus Christ.

Henry David Thoreau said, "I should not talk so much about myself if there were anybody else whom I knew as well" (*Walden,* "Economy"). Thoreau thereby provides ample justification for the personal nature of this book. I am reading the story of David in the light of my own experience with brothers in the journey of faith. The suggestions for "Time Out" are a direct response to the friend who read the manuscript and said, "Okay, so how do I do this?" My hope is that these practical suggestions for exploring your spirituality will enable you to experience the Spirit of God at work in your life. To this end, I have provided some of the tools you will need; it will be up to you to take the necessary time out required for careful thought, reflection/discussion, spiritual examination, and prayer.

I do not assume that every reader is a signed-and-sealed, church-going, Bible-reading, promise-keeping Christian. The imaginary faces of potential readers that gather around my computer screen as I write include men who are not ready to sign on to the historic creeds of the faith, but who feel a fire in their belly—or at least a warm flame—ignited by the image of manhood revealed in Jesus Christ. My hope is that as we see the way God was at work in the life of David, we will discover new ways in which God may be at work in our lives, and that we will be led to a life filled with robust passion, spiritual power, and joyful praise.

> Thou who art over us,
> Thou who art one of us,
> Thou who *art*—
> Also within us,
> May all see Thee—in me also . . .
>
> Give me a pure heart—that I may see Thee,
> A humble heart—that I may hear Thee,
> A heart of love—that I may serve Thee,
> A heart of faith—that I may abide in Thee.

(Dag Hammarskjöld, *Markings*, New York: Knopf, 1964, p. 100)

Chapter One

Calling

Finding the Man
God Created You to Be

1 Samuel 16:1-13

The longest journey
Is the journey inwards.
—*Dag Hammarskjöld*, Markings

Tucked away in the back room of my male identity is the memory of a specific corner of adolescent hell known as seventh-grade gym class. By testing it on a wide variety of men's groups, I've discovered that a high percentage of the male population shares the memory with me. If you identify with this bit of personal history, you probably need to be reassured that you weren't alone. If you were among the genetically favored few who inherited perfect bodies and fully matured adolescent egos with the first explosion of your glands, you probably need to be informed about what the rest of us experienced!

We would line up along the side of the field, our pubescent bodies clad in gym uniforms that were designed either by a very well-built high-school senior with a very sick sense of humor or by a sadistic adult who really hated kids. Gym uniforms were always far too small on the overweight kids and too large on the underweight ones, ensuring that everyone's physical defects were put on spectacular display. The few guys who looked good in them were the ones who looked great in anything. We were fully capable of imagining that every girl in the school was peeking out of the Home Economics classroom window, laughing at most of us and lusting for a few of us. The difference between their laughter and their lust was determined by our athletic prowess and our lack of pimples.

Our "No Guts, No Glory" coach would choose the two best athletes in the class to be captains. They would pick their teams, alternating back and forth, choosing one kid at a time. The one whose name was called would line up behind his new captain. It goes without saying that the captains always chose the best athletes first, ensuring that the kids who had not been in training since kindergarten to be voted "Most Athletic" in the senior class were left standing in uniform-clad humiliation along the field. Our value declined in direct proportion to the length of time it took for us to be chosen. I was invariably the kid at the end of the line, my twin brother beside me, providing a Harnish for each team. Wherever you were along that line, the lesson we learned was simple and clear: Our value was measured by an externally applied standard that had nothing to do with what was going on inside our awkward, adolescent bodies.

It's still true. I am now a middle-aged, emotionally healthy, physically active guy who works out at the "Y" and has discovered that on the other side of fifty, being skinny isn't so bad! But the memory is still tucked away, deep within the person I have become. We may have left seventh-grade gym class far behind, but our manhood is constantly being measured, judged, and valued by all sorts of external standards: the shape of our body, the style (or amount!) of our hair, the title on our door, the model of our car, the color of our skin, the size of our bank account. The world measures our manhood from the outside in.

Remember when manufacturers' labels were hidden on the inside of clothing? Coming home from J.C. Penney's on Main Street, we would have been embarrassed to discover that the label was sticking out from the collar of the shirt or the waistband of our pants. It's not that way anymore. Everyone wants Tommy Hilfiger's name on everything. Put a Ralph Lauren label on a shirt and you can double the price. Even when I buy such clothing on the discount table, I wonder how much I'm paying for the clothing and how much I'm investing in what I hope other people think when they see me with the label. It probably still has something to do with being that kid at the end of the line.

If you've been there with me, take heart! That's where we find David in the beginning of his story. He was the kid at the end of the line. The Lord sent Samuel, the chief prophet and king-maker, to Bethlehem, to the house of Jesse, to anoint one of Jesse's sons as the future king. That sounded simple enough. Samuel knew how to pick a king. He had chosen Saul, the first king of Israel, of whom it was said, "There was not a man among the people of Israel more handsome than he; he stood head and shoulders above everyone else" (1 Samuel 9:2).

Jesse trotted out his firstborn son, a strapping hunk name Eliab. One look at him and Samuel knew he had found his man. Samuel was ready to pour the anointing oil on Eliab's head when God whispered in his ear, "Do not look on his appearance or on the height of his stature, because I have rejected him" (1 Samuel 16:7). Oops! So much for Eliab. One by one, Jesse paraded his sons in front of the prophet. Samuel took a good look at each one, listened for the voice of God, and passed on them like a quiz show host eliminating contestants. "Sorry, Abinadab; it's not you, but thanks for playing!" "Good try, Shammah, but it's not you, either! You can pick up your consolation prize at the door."

Finally, Samuel asked Jesse, "Are all your sons here?" (1 Samuel 16:11). Jesse must have scratched his balding head and thought for a moment. I imagine him saying, "Well, come to think of it, there is one more. We left him with the sheep. You probably wouldn't be interested in him, anyway. Let's see, what did we name him? [David's name is never mentioned in this passage.] Say, wouldn't you like to take another look at Eliab?"

Samuel told Jesse to track down the boy who had been left with the sheep. When David was brought in, Samuel saw something no one else had noticed: "He was ruddy, and had beautiful eyes, and was handsome" (1 Samuel 16:12a). God enabled Samuel to see things in David that no one else had seen. God revealed the hidden potential for greatness in this kid who had been left at the end of the line.

"Rise and anoint him," the Lord said, "for this is the one." As the oil was being poured over David's adolescent head, "the spirit of the LORD came mightily upon David from that day forward" (1 Samuel 16:13). This largely unseen action of God set in motion a whole new destiny for David's life. God had chosen this insignificant shepherd boy as the one through whom God's purpose would be accomplished. The writer might as well have put the moral of the story in flashing lights on the side of the Goodyear blimp:

The LORD does not see as mortals see; they look on the outward appearance, but the LORD looks on the heart. (1 Samuel 16:7)

Popular author and motivational speaker Stephen Covey has repackaged the principle in this Bible story for our time. In his book *The Seven Habits of Highly Effective People,* he defines his "principle-centered, character-based" approach to personal and interpersonal effectiveness as an "inside-out" approach to life: " 'Inside-out' means to start first with self; even more fundamentally, to start with the most *inside* part of self—with your paradigms, your character, and your motives" (New York: Simon and Schuster, 1989, pp. 42-43).

Covey says that he has never seen genuine happiness or success come from the outside in; it always emerges from the inside out. He reaffirms what God revealed to Samuel more than a thousand years before the birth of Christ: What matters most in life is not outward appearance, but the inner realities of the human heart.

Spirituality—a term that may sound either strangely spooky or uncomfortably effeminate to some men—begins with a commitment to look at life from the inside out. It is a disciplined response to a gnawing dissatisfaction with the "outside in" approach to life. It meets the soul-hunger of a media executive who wrote in a letter to me:

One area that I am seeing among those baby-booming, hitting-50, what's-happening-to-my-body, my-kids-are-adults, how's-my-401K-doing, I'm-too-young-to-be-this-old guys, is finding peace of mind. Most of us have spent our life busting our ass to succeed in those things that we either have an obligation to or "think" measure a person's success or happiness. For many, it has been a life filled with frustration, because we either have been told or convinced ourselves, it's never good enough. Now, we are beginning to see the light (much of it reflecting off the top of our heads). We haven't left much time for ourselves, or for our friends, or family, or God. I don't think most men have the same unrealistic expectations of their lives that drove them in their 30s, but they still want it all to "mean" something, to have value: A peace of mind that they have made, and can continue to make, a difference. There's a common thread of putting your true priorities in order and living them in harmony with your faith.

By *spirituality,* I mean the way the Spirit of God is at work within the deep, inner core of our being to accomplish God's purpose for our lives. For a follower of Jesus Christ, spirituality is the process by which the way, will, words, and life of Jesus become a living reality that shapes our lives from the inside out. It is the discipline by which we order our lives around a central commitment to Jesus Christ.

The apostle Paul described the process of spiritual formation when he prayed "that you may be filled with the knowledge of God's will in all spiritual wisdom and understanding, so that you may lead lives worthy of the Lord, fully pleasing to him, as you bear fruit in every good work" (Colossians 1:9*b*-10). Paul clearly overstretched the boundary of male experience when he said, "I am again in the pain of childbirth until Christ is formed in you" (Galatians 4:19). My wife would justifiably ask, "What does *he* know about childbirth?" But Paul's statement is a graphic illustration of the depth of his desire for his friends to experience life from the inside out, life that is shaped in the way, words, and spirit of Jesus Christ.

Because of this "inside out" approach, the God of the Bible has a strange way of choosing people who, by the world's standards, would be left at the end of the line:

- By outward appearance, Moses was a stuttering fugitive who was hiding out in the desert, but God looked on his heart and saw the one who would lead the children of Israel to freedom.
- Esther was the slave-queen of a pagan king, but God looked on her heart and saw the woman who would save the nation.
- Joseph was a poor carpenter from a nowhere place called Nazareth, but God looked on his heart and saw the one who would be the human parent for the Christ child.
- Simon was a loudmouthed, bull-headed, undependable fisherman, but God looked on his heart and named him Peter, the rock upon which the early church would be built.

You can track the same pattern of God's call in the lives of men and women throughout history:

- By outward appearance, Martin Luther was a guilt-ridden monk in search of his own salvation, but God looked on his heart and saw the man who would lead a Reformation.
- John Wesley was a stuffy Anglican priest who had failed as a mis-

sionary to America, but God looked on his heart and saw the one who could ignite a spiritual awakening in England and give birth to the Methodist movement.

- Martin Luther King, Jr., was just another preacher's kid in Atlanta, but God looked on his heart and saw the drum major for freedom in America.
- Mother Teresa was a diminutive nun in an insignificant convent in Albania, but God looked on her heart and saw the woman who would model Christian compassion for the last half of the twentieth century.
- Desmond Tutu was an altar boy in an Anglican church in South Africa, but God looked on his heart and saw the spiritual leader who would help birth a new nation.

The world judged all of them from the outside in, but God looked on their hearts and released the hidden potential within them.

It is no coincidence that God's call came to David in early adolescence, long before anyone else saw any sign of greatness within him. Many of us begin to sense our inner calling during our adolescent search for our own identity. Our childhood experiences of affirmation and self-worth become the internal gyroscope around which our lives revolve. They continue to influence us.

In her Pulitzer Prize-winning biography of Franklin and Eleanor Roosevelt, Doris Kearns Goodwin described "the ambience of boundless devotion that encompassed [Franklin] as a child." She concluded that "the sense of being loved wholeheartedly by his parents taught Roosevelt to trust that the world was basically a friendly and agreeable place" (*No Ordinary Time*, New York: Simon and Schuster, 1994, pp. 74-75). Goodwin points to Roosevelt's sense of self-worth as the deep, inner source of the strength that enabled him to lead the United States out of the Great Depression and through World War II.

In a similar way, Leslie Weatherhead described a boyhood day when his mother sent him to the market for vegetables. Looking at his reflection above the cabbages and carrots in a shop window, he remembered saying aloud, "I could be great for Christ" (*Leslie Weatherhead: A Personal Portrait*, Nashville: Abingdon Press, 1975, p. 22). From that first inkling of God's call, Weatherhead became the spiritual voice of British Methodism in the first half of this century, and the impact of his writings continues today. You'll find that same kind of adolescent awareness in the lives of men like John Wesley, Abraham Lincoln, and Martin Luther King, Jr.

Other people discover their sense of calling over time. Nelson Mandela said that "no epiphany, no singular revelation, no moment of truth" shaped his life purpose. Rather, he said, "a steady accumulation of a thousand slights, a thousand indignities, a thousand unremembered moments, produced in me an anger, a rebelliousness, a desire to fight the system that imprisoned my people. There was no particular day on which I said, From henceforth I will devote myself to the liberation of my people; instead, I simply found myself doing so, and could not do otherwise" (*Long Walk To Freedom,* Boston: Little, Brown, and Co., 1994, p. 83).

A calling is an inner awareness that God has a divine purpose for our existence. It is a deep sense of being "at home" with the person we are becoming. It is a maturing consciousness of our value as a person created in God's image, redeemed by God's love, and chosen by God for the abundant life that Jesus said he came to bring.

God's unique calling for David's life came through the prophet Samuel, even as it had come to Samuel through an elderly priest named Eli (1 Samuel 3). Most of us, I suspect, sense God's destiny for our lives through personal mentors with prophetic sensitivity who release the hidden possibilities within us.

While attending a denominational conference, I was impressed by a dignified man who simply "took the room" when he walked in. His sense of personal presence clearly came from the inside out and involved more than just his physical appearance. Turning to the pastor-friend beside me, I said, "Wow, does that guy have style!" She replied, "He must have had a very good mother!"

She got it right. After that man became my friend, he told me how his childhood faith had been nurtured by a faithful mother who, in spite of great hardship, taught him that he was loved and valued as a child of God. He described the little Methodist congregation that encouraged and supported him. His inner sense of calling was the product of their nurture and care.

Looking back to the days when I was a scrawny seventh-grader at the end of the line, I vividly recall feelings of soul-searing inadequacy reinforced by experiences of painful rejection and humiliation from my peers. I, too, had a very good mother and a very good father. They gave their sons unbounded affirmation and support. The other place I found that kind of affirmation was in the church.

The picture album in my soul contains the memories of people at First United Methodist Church in Clarion, Pennsylvania, who let me know that I was a valuable person, even when I acted like an adolescent jerk! I can hear the voices of Sunday school teachers, youth counselors, and summer youth camp preachers who saw possibilities within me that I could not see. I remember a retired pastor who placed his gnarled hands on mine and prayed that I'd become a preacher. I can recount the opportunities for leadership my church family opened for me. In their love, I experienced the love of God. Their affirmation of the hidden possibilities within my life shaped God's call for me.

God's choice of David is good news for adolescent kids who feel as if they have been left at the end of the line. It also offers good news for adults who bear the scars of hurts that were inflicted upon them when they were young. The awareness that God looks on the heart offers good news for all who feel that they have been led down a dead-end street by the "outside in" way of the world around us and are searching for spiritual reality that shapes life from the inside out. The promise that God continues to see things within us that no one else sees means that throughout our lives the Spirit of God continues to set us free from the past and release us for new possibilities in the future.

The story of David's calling also challenges each of us to become a "Samuel" to some young "David." More than one-half of the children in America today spend some part of their childhood in a single-parent home. Most of these children have to deal with the reality of an "absentee father." It is critically important for spiritually sensitive men to become prophetic mentors through whom God's purpose can be affirmed in these young men's lives.

I keep in my file a copy of a letter written by Linda Wells for her son, Talley, when he graduated from Duke University. Linda described a day in early adolescence when she discovered a well-worn Bible in Talley's bathroom. She had no idea that he had become a regular Bible-reader, but she was quite certain that reading material that achieves bathroom status should be taken seriously. Linda wrote that "finding the Bible confirmed a conviction I had developed at an earlier point, that Talley was marked by faith; that what Talley knew and believed and sensed and shared was, to the best of my ability to find meaning in the term, a 'calling.' "

Enclosed with the letter was a photograph of the confirmation class at St. Luke's United Methodist Church, which also included my wife's and my oldest daughter, Carrie. Linda recounted the way my voice had cracked and my tears had flowed as I placed a cross around my daughter's neck and confirmed her in "the faith and fellowship of all true disciples of Jesus Christ." She described the way my tears gave permission to the rest of the congregation to weep with joy over the offspring of that church's faith. She also described the role that confirmation class played in her son's life.

> At a time when, as a teenager, life is full of uncertainty and pain and self-consciousness, something very important happens among those kinds of friends. Maybe it is the increased self-confidence; maybe the assurance that you can be silly and still faithful, goofy and still a child of God, fun-loving and loved.

I was grateful to be named in the "line of prophets and saints who have enriched Talley's experience." As Linda wrote, "I believe that Talley learned from [you] that kind of questioning which values human beings and values human intelligence and beings from strong, Christian-based assumptions about what is right and just and good."

Talley is an adult now. We recently celebrated his marriage. Several years ago he and I wrestled together with the possibility that God might be calling him into the ordained ministry. Instead, God has led him to follow his father into the law. Only God knows where his future will lead, but his identity was formed around a sense of calling that grew out of a family that lived its faith, a Bible in his bathroom, and a confirmation class more than a decade ago. And that calling began to shape his life from the inside out.

During a recent trip to Boston, I had my picture taken beside the marvelous statue of Phillips Brooks that stands in the courtyard of Trinity Church, looking out on Copley Square. During his years as the pastor of that congregation, Brooks became one of the prophetic voices of nineteenth-century America. In my favorite Brooks story, he invited his congregation to imagine a great artist walking down the streets of Boston. Coming upon a house with a large window, the artist looked inside and saw an easel. On the easel there was a large canvas, and beside the easel, a table loaded down with brushes and paint in every imaginable color. Then Brooks invited his congregation to imagine the artist saying, "Ah, what a masterpiece I could paint if only I could get inside."

"Spirituality" is nothing more or less than the process by which we allow the Spirit of God to get inside our human personality and begin to fulfill God's calling for us from the inside out.

Praise the LORD!
. . . .

His delight is not in the strength of the horse,
    nor his pleasure in the speed of a runner;
but the LORD takes pleasure in those who fear him,
    in those who hope in his steadfast love.
(Psalm 147:1, 10-11)

Time Out

C
A
L
L
I
N
G

A guy in my congregation has a genuine calling to connect spiritually searching people with Jesus Christ. When he describes the way that connection has happened in his life, he talks about a series of "defining moments" when he became aware of God's presence and responded in commitment to Christ. You could also call them "divine moments" when we experience a personal connection with Jesus Christ. The suggestions offered here may help you experience those defining moments in your life. You may wish to keep a personal journal or notebook as you move through this process. Along the way, I hope that the defining moments will also be divine moments for you.

1. *Look at David.* Read 1 Samuel 16:1-13. Where can you identify with David in this story?

2. *Look at your past.* What were some of the defining adolescent experiences that shaped your emerging self-concept? How do those memories continue to influence your life? As a teenager, did you have any sense of God's presence in your life? Who were the Samuel figures who loved, affirmed, and guided you?

3. *Look at your life today.* What's in your heart? What will it mean for you to live more fully from the inside out, rather than living from the outside in?

4. *Look at your relationship with God.* How have you felt God's love for you? What hidden possibilities does God see inside your life?

C
A
L
L
I
N
G

5. *Invite Jesus in.* Spend a few moments in silence with these words from the risen Christ: "Listen! I am standing at the door, knocking; if you hear my voice and open the door, I will come in to you and eat with you, and you with me" (Revelation 3:20). Picture your inner life as a house. Imagine that Jesus is standing at the door. Hear him knocking. As an act of response to God's love, invite Jesus to come into your life the way you would invite a guest to come into your house.

6. *Prayer.* In your own words, try praying something like this: "Lord, I've seen you 'out there' in the lives of others. I've sensed your presence in worship. I've heard your words through the Scriptures. Now, I really want to know you inside, not as a visitor, but as a permanent resident in my life. I want you to define my inner sense of who I am. I want you to guide my life from the inside out. So, Lord, I open the door of my inner self to you and pray that you will keep your promise and come in. Let me know your presence, and begin your work in me. Thank you, Lord. Welcome home!"

Healing

Songs for the Troubled Soul

1 Samuel 16:14-23

Jesus acts as a tuning fork to the Creator, the Eternal. If we would seek to get our own lives back in tune with God, it must be through listening to Christ's frequencies and matching the resonance of our actions and attitudes to Jesus' pitch.

—*Leonard I. Sweet*, Homiletic, *January–March 1997*

I have a friend who is like a whole lot of guys I've known in every community I've served. He is bright, energetic, and has a great family. He's doing very well in his career. Every time I run into him he has just purchased another new toy: the best ski boat, a flashy sports car, a home on the water, a big-screen television. You name it, he's got it. He's a fitness fanatic and is built like a Kentucky thoroughbred. He designed a fully equipped exercise room into his new office. He plays tennis, golf, and softball and plans his work schedule around trips to Colorado to snow ski in the winter. We laugh a lot; he has a delightful—if just a little obscene—sense of humor. He works hard and, by all outward standards, has fulfilled the secular version of "the American dream." I really like this guy! From the outside in, he is doing just fine.

But I remember the day he received word that one of his tennis buddies had been diagnosed with cancer. The news cracked my friend's macho façade. He told me he was really scared. "If this guy can get cancer," he said, "it could happen to any of us!" On the inside, my friend was afraid of getting old, scared of death, and absolutely petrified at the thought of losing his physical and sexual powers. He confessed that his addiction to exercise was his attempt to fight off the possibility of death. He was beginning to face his hunger for inner, spiritual wholeness, which could never be satisfied by the external stuff he had acquired.

My friend is not unique. He is, in fact, typical of men who have been conditioned by the "outside in" addiction of our culture. Eugene Peterson, widely respected as a writer and professor of spiritual theology, says that the exponentially expanding interest in spirituality in our country today is "more likely to be evidence of pathology than health. . . . The interest itself is not sick, but sickness has provoked the interest." Although there is considerable confusion about the cure, he says, there is widespread agreement on the ailment: "Our culture is sick with secularism" (*Subversive Spirituality,* Grand Rapids: Eerdmans, 1997, p. 32). We've tried living without a spiritual center, but life has turned out to be relationally empty, spiritually hollow, and utterly incapable of healing the deepest hungers, hurts, and fears of our souls.

King Saul was a lot like many of us. He had all the trappings of success, but he was depressed, tormented, frightened, and alone. He was a man with a deeply troubled soul.

Some say Saul was paranoid, controlled by a paralyzing fear that someone was out to take away his power. What man has not been frozen with fear? Who hasn't been anxious when corporate chieftains talk about "re-engineering" or "downsizing"? Who hasn't been afraid when his leadership is threatened by powerful forces that he cannot control? Who isn't afraid of physical weakness, sexual impotence, or death?

Some say Saul suffered from emotional depression. What man, if he is honest with himself, has not been depressed? Who among us has not known days when he felt as if he were flying with the eagles, only to be followed by nights when he didn't think he had the energy to waddle with the ducks? Who hasn't had the blues?

Some say Saul was jealous. There's no indication that Saul had a clue about Samuel's clandestine trip to Jesse's house to anoint David as the future king, but it was impossible to miss the warmhearted, good-looking, unusually gifted boy from Bethlehem. What man is not stabbed by the purple pang of jealousy when someone else gets the promotion he thought he was in line to receive; when he sees the ease with which another guy sinks that impossible putt; when all those guys on the beach with perfectly toned bodies make him even more aware of the imperfections of his own?

We know Saul was consumed by guilt. His story had begun so well.

When Samuel anointed him and laid his hands on Saul's head, God's presence was so real, so vibrant, so alive within him that it was as if Saul could hear God speaking directly into his ear. But Saul blatantly disobeyed what he knew to be the will of God (see 1 Samuel 15). Samuel declared that because Saul had rejected the Lord's command, the Lord had rejected him. Saul's soul was empty. The directing, guiding, motivating power of God's presence within him evaporated. He was a hollow hulk of a man, depressed, jealous, and afraid. The biblical writer described Saul's decline in one terrifying line: "Now the spirit of the LORD departed from Saul, and an evil spirit from the LORD tormented him" (1 Samuel 16:14).

The Bible does not say that God is the source of evil; but the Bible *does* say that when God's goodness is rejected, evil is all that is left. The Bible says that we are created to live with the Spirit of God within us. Take that Spirit away, and the soul is empty. When God is no longer the organizing center of human experience, we are destined for confusion, darkness, and despair. And that's where we find Saul: tormented, depressed, guilty, afraid.

Everyone could see that in spite of everything he had, Saul was a mess. That's when one of the servants suggested that music might help. Nineteen centuries later, a British poet named William Congreve would give us the familiar prescription "Music hath charms to soothe the savage breast." But someone in Saul's court had heard that Jesse's son spent his time in the hills writing poetry in the morning sunlight and singing songs beneath the stars. They brought David to the court, and whenever the evil spirits tormented Saul, David would sing his songs, and Saul's soul would again be at peace.

We know some of the songs David sang. Tradition tells us that many of the psalms were his. Try to imagine how Saul must have felt in his darkest hours when he heard David sing:

> The LORD is my shepherd, I shall not want.
> He makes me lie down in green pastures;
> he leads me beside still waters;
> he restores my soul.
>
> . . . .
> Even though I walk through the darkest valley,
> I fear no evil;
> for you are with me. (Psalm 23:1-3*a*, 4)

When Saul was frozen with fear, I like to imagine how it felt for him to hear David's voice singing

> The LORD is my light and my salvation;
> whom shall I fear?
> The LORD is the stronghold of my life;
> of whom shall I be afraid?
> . . . .
> Though an army encamp against me,
> my heart shall not fear. (Psalm 27:1, 3a)

When the clouds of depression closed in around the king, he may have heard David recite the poem that says

> I was on my way to the depths below,
> but you restored my life.
>
> Sing praise to the LORD,
> all his faithful people!
> Remember what the Holy One has done.
> . . . .
> His anger lasts only a moment,
> his goodness for a lifetime.
> Tears may flow in the night,
> but joy comes in the morning. (Psalm 30:3-5 TEV)

When Saul's guilt overwhelmed him and he questioned whether there was any hope of forgiveness, I am sure David reminded him,

> Happy are those whose sins are forgiven,
> whose wrongs are pardoned.
> . . . .
> When I did not confess my sins,
> I was worn out from crying all day long.
> . . . .
> My strength was completely drained,
> as moisture is dried up by the summer heat.
>
> Then I confessed my sins to you;
> . . . .
> and you forgave all my sins. (Psalm 32:1-5 TEV)

And when the darkness passed, and the light of God's goodness began to shine again, I hope Saul learned to sing

> Bless the LORD, O my soul,
>   and all that is within me,
>   bless his holy name.
> Bless the LORD, O my soul,
>   and do not forget all his benefits—
> who forgives all your iniquity,
>   who heals all your diseases,
> who redeems your life from the Pit,
>   who crowns you with steadfast love and mercy . . .
>   so that your strength is renewed like the eagle's.
>
> (Psalm 103:1-4, 5*b*)

You don't have to know how to read a note of music or how to play anything other than the radio to understand the effect David's music had on Saul. It is a vivid picture of the way the Spirit of God brings order, harmony, and peace to the troubled places in the inner depths of our souls. Spiritual discipline is the process by which I tune my spirit to the Spirit of God. It is the way I allow the Spirit of Jesus to bring order and harmony to my confused, troubled, frightened existence.

Legend has it that when novelist Lloyd C. Douglas was a university student, he lived in a boarding house where an old musician lived on the first floor. Douglas and the old man developed a daily ritual. On his way down the stairs, Douglas would open the old man's door, stick his head into the room, and ask, "Well, what's the good news today?" The old man would pick up his tuning fork, strike it on the arm of his wheelchair, and listen for the tone. He would announce, "That's middle C. The tenor upstairs sings flat, the piano across the hall is out of tune, but that, my friend, is middle C. It was middle C yesterday; it will be middle C tomorrow; it will still be middle C a thousand years from now. That's middle C!" The purpose of spiritual discipline is to tune our lives to Jesus as the "middle C" of human experience so that he becomes the constant, healing reality at the center of our existence.

But how does that healing process happen in our lives? To answer that question, I want to invite you to imagine that the music David played for Saul was jazz. Okay, I know I'm stretching your imagination, but when I read this story I hear the blues. Imagine that you were in the crowd of more than a thousand people who filled the nave of the National Cathedral in Washington, D.C., on Martin Luther King, Jr., Day in 1996. They came to hear Wynton Marsalis, the wunderkind of modern jazz, present a two-hour service entitled "In This House, On This Morning." In an interview about the service, Marsalis called blues jazz "a healing agent for the soul." He said the music gives a person who is in pain "a broader vision of life, of reality. It makes you humble. And it can lift you up all at the same time." Marsalis said, "It all starts with God . . . and it returns to God. It's a matter between the musician and God just as it's a matter between the listener and God" (Robert A. Becker, "Blues Jazz and Spirituality," *Cathedral Age*, Summer 1997, pp. 16-17).

The process by which we experience God's presence within our souls follows the pattern of African American worship upon which Marsalis designed the jazz service in the National Cathedral. The service began with a mournful, piercing wail from the soprano sax. It was the cry of the longing, hurting soul. The healing process begins with that kind of longing for God. If the ailment of our souls is a lack of God's presence in the center of our being, then the cure can only be found by turning our attention away from ourselves and in the direction of the God whom we so desperately need. It begins in the lonely cry of one who is honest enough to acknowledge his need, his hurt, his pain. The first step in the healing process is to name the longing within, to identify the specific way in which we need to experience God's healing presence.

In the next movement of the jazz service, the penetrating sound of a trumpet echoed through the cathedral as the voice of the preacher proclaiming the word. Like the sound of a trumpet, the words of scripture define our longing and announce the coming of the God who brings healing. The next step in the healing process is to listen for the living Word through the words of the Bible.

From a Christian perspective, it is impossible to overemphasize our need to keep our spiritual experience rooted in scripture. Vague "spirituality" can easily degenerate into shallow navel-gazing. An overly subjective religious experience can easily become little more than a neurotic fascination with what is going on in our guts. It may evolve into a neurotic level of self-absorption that reeks of a pretentious self-righteousness in which our experience becomes the sacred text of spiritual reality. The only antidote for the sickness of self-absorption is to turn our attention away from ourselves and onto the wholeness of life revealed in Jesus Christ. The authoritative text for Christian spirituality is not our subjective experience but God's self-revelation recorded in the Bible.

The cathedral service continued with a movement of prayer that Marsalis called a "dialogue with God." Prayer is conversation with God. It is the way we learn to speak out of the deep places in our soul and listen for the sound of the Spirit moving within. Prayer is the discipline by which we bring each part of our personality into harmony with the perfect pitch of God's intention for us revealed in Jesus.

I used to think that prayer had a lot to do with my mouth. It was the way I told God what I wanted or filled God in on how to run things down here on earth. It was the process by which I made my shopping list for God to fill at the heavenly K-Mart. But that has changed. I've come to realize that prayer has more to do with my ears than with my mouth. It is the quiet space in which I listen for God to speak in the deep places of my soul. It is the silence in which I hear—not audibly from the outside in, but spiritually from the inside out—the will of God for my life. Out of that deep listening, I enter into dialogue with God about the very real, mundane, practical concerns of my life and my world.

Marsalis's jazz service then moved to the "altar call." The altar call is the invitation for each of us to surrender ourselves in response to the claim of God in our lives. We are always free to choose to continue to respond to the healing presence or to return to the "dis-ease" of disharmonious living, just the way we are always able to choose the healthy path of exercise or the unhealthy life of a couch potato. Healing comes through surrender to the wholeness of God's presence within us. New life comes through practical obedience to the will of God. I'll confess that most of the time my problem is not that I cannot discover the will of God, but that I'm not willing to obey what I already know!

The Old Testament describes Naaman as "a great man," a commander in the army, a man with authority and power. But he was also afflicted with leprosy. When Naaman came to the prophet Elijah for healing, Elijah told him to dip himself seven times in the Jordan river. This directive offended Naaman; it really ticked him off. He had expected Elijah to perform a spectacular act of healing—like one of those TV evangelists, I guess—so that everyone would notice and applaud. Heck, he had better-looking rivers back home, Naaman must have thought. He wasn't about to wade into the Jordan! But one of his servants suggested, "If the prophet had commanded you to do something difficult, would you not have done it? How much more, when all he said to you was, 'Wash, and be clean'?" (2 Kings 5:13). Naaman reluctantly obeyed, probably not really expecting much to happen. But as soon as he came out of the water, "his flesh was restored like the flesh of a young boy, and he was clean" (2 Kings 5:14). Here's the point of Naaman's story: Healing comes through practical obedience to what we know of the will of God. Though we never know God's will completely, we can know enough to take the next step of obedience and begin walking in the way of Jesus Christ.

Like the jazz service in the cathedral, our movement toward wholeness leads us into harmony with other spiritual pilgrims. Describing what happens for jazz musicians, Marsalis said, "It's a very intense art form . . . there's a spiritual bonding going on up there. . . . So it takes humility. If you can't have humility to be in balance with others, you won't be as good as you might be" ("Blues Jazz and Spirituality," p. 17). Along the path toward spiritual wholeness, our lives become intertwined with others, just the way the jazz musicians in the cathedral wove their music into one another and drew the congregation along with them. Healing comes through community. We cannot be made whole and remain alone.

In recent years a number of people have shared with me the story of their experiences in Alcoholics Anonymous. Although their healing began when they acknowledged their need, the healing is being accomplished in company with other people in need. Not one of them could have found sobriety alone. Their continued health is utterly dependent on their continued connection with their brothers and sisters in the healing process.

The jazz service in the cathedral ended on a note of exuberant praise that reverberated through the nave and filled the lives of the people in the congregation. In the same way, the healing process moves toward praise in which we realize the freedom of wholeness and give thanks to God. There is healing in worship; there is strength in corporate praise; there is soul-cleansing grace in the water of baptism and soul-nourishing food in the bread and cup of Holy Communion.

A newspaper reporter visited our contemporary worship service to find out what was going on at Hyde Park Church that was attracting so many unchurched folks. She told the readers of *The St. Petersburg Times,* "People aren't just attending . . . they seem to be responding. There are quiet snuffles each week, a rustling of men looking for handkerchiefs to hide tears and women crying softly." The reporter quoted one worshiper who said, "I have so many emotional wounds, and I get healed a little bit each week." It defined the healing power of corporate worship in the lives of people who are searching for new life (*St. Petersburg Times,* August 4, 1996, p. 6F).

I realize, of course, that jazz was not actually the music Saul heard. But David's music brought healing to Saul's troubled soul the way Wynton Marsalis's music touched the souls of people in the cathedral. Whatever David's tune, the healing song we desperately need is not some giddy, inconsequential little ditty that dances across the very real pain, the gut-wrenching hurt, the incapacitating fear, the frigid loneliness that men rarely acknowledge but often feel. Instead, it is music that emerges out of the depths of the human soul. It is the music that moves to the rhythm of God's deep, abiding love. It is soul-music that takes into itself every part of our life and transforms it into a song of praise.

> Out of the depths I cry to you, O LORD.
>   Lord, hear my voice!
>
> . . . .
>
> O Israel, hope in the LORD!
>   For with the LORD there is steadfast love,
> and with him is great power to redeem.
>   (Psalm 130: 1-2*a*, 7)

Time Out

H
E
A
L
I
N
G

1. *Listen for the healing music.* A practical way to begin is by reading the psalms in a contemporary translation. I recommend the New Revised Standard Version or *The Message,* a contemporary paraphrase by Eugene Peterson. Listen for the emotions. When you find a psalm that identifies with your feelings, take time to listen, reflect, and meditate upon it.

2. *Follow the pattern.* Walk through the movements of Wynton Marsalis's jazz service and ask these questions:

   - What is the deepest longing in my soul? Can I name the thing that troubles me? Am I listening for God's word through the Bible?
   - Have I learned to enter into dialogue with God through prayer?
   - Where do I need to bring my life into harmony with the will of God? What is the new surrender to which God is calling me?
   - Have I found a trusted friend, a spiritual counselor, or a supportive group of spiritual pilgrims with whom I can share my search for healing?
   - Am I discovering the strength that comes from the discipline of corporate worship? Have I found the healing that comes through praise?

3. *Tune your soul to Jesus.* Read the Gospel of Luke. Walk the dusty paths of human experience with Jesus. Find yourself in his story. Look for how the words, way, and love of Jesus connect with your inner hunger. Allow this Jesus to become the "tuning fork" for your life from the inside out.

H
E
A
L
I
N
G

4. *Prayer.* Spend some quiet time reflecting on these words from an eleventh-century theologian named Anselm:

Come now, little child.
Turn awhile from your daily work;
hide yourself for a little time from your restless thoughts,
cast away your troublesome cares;
put aside your wearisome distractions.
Give yourself a little leisure to talk with God,
and rest awhile in him.
Enter the secret chamber of your heart,
shutting out everything but God,
and that which may help you in seeking him.
And when you've closed the door, seek him.
Now, my whole heart, say to God:
. . . .
I will seek you by desiring you,
and desire you in seeking you.
I will find you by loving you,
and love you in finding you.
. . . .
I do not seek to understand so that I may believe,
but believe that I may understand.
For this I know to be true:
that unless I first believe I shall not understand.

St. Anselm, 1033–1109
(in *The English Spirit,*
Nashville: Abingdon Press, 1988, p. 16)

Chapter Three

Faith

How to Slay
a Giant

1 Samuel 17

> Always be sure that you struggle with Christian methods
> and Christian weapons . . . using only the weapon of love.
>
> —*Martin Luther King, Jr., "The Most Durable Power"*

I might as well begin this chapter as cantankerously as possible by sharing my conviction that when it comes down to it, a whole lot of creed-affirming, church-going, Bible-believing, offering-plate-passing folks are doctrinal theists and practical atheists. Ask us what we believe, and ninety-something percent of us will say we believe in God. Those of us who hang around churches on Sunday morning will be even more specific. We will say that we believe in the God whose story is told in the Bible and who was revealed in Jesus. We may even say that we believe in the Sermon on the Mount or the central affirmations of the Christian faith expressed in the Apostles' Creed. On Sunday, we are doctrinal theists. From the outside in, we look like people who actually believe in God.

But Monday morning comes, and in the ordinary, day-to-day actions of our lives, we become practical atheists. We live as if the God in whom we say we believe has made a quick exit stage right, leaving us behind to perform the rest of the drama alone. We function as if we were here to work things out on the basis of our own human wisdom and strength. We say we believe in an infinite God, but when we wrestle with the giants in our own lives, we act as if all we have going for us are our finite, human wits and powers. The faith we claim on Sunday has no apparent influence on the way we treat the people with whom we work during the week. The creed we affirm in worship does not determine the values by which decisions are made. The call to love the Lord our God with all our heart, soul, mind, and strength and to love others the way Jesus loved us does not condition our words, actions, and relationships. If a spiritual life were a contagious disease like the flu, no one we met along the street would need to worry about catching it from us. In terms of the practical ways our beliefs influence our behavior from the inside out, we might as well be atheists.

A woman in Fort Lauderdale, Florida, did a random survey of the restaurants within a mile of two of the largest congregations in the state. She asked the table servers what day of the week was the most difficult for them. They all agreed it was Sunday, when the restaurants are filled with folks coming from worship. "They are lousy tippers," table servers told the survey taker. "They can be very demanding, and some are downright mean." The servers know doctrinal theists and practical atheists when they serve them!

So, let's ask a very basic question. Is there a God who is actively involved in human history or are we here to slug it out on our own? Is there a God who is at work in the turmoil, confusion, tension, and con-flict of our world to accomplish a redemptive purpose, or are we here to make the best we can of it? Is there a God who will, to the degree to which we make ourselves available, use us to fulfill that redemptive purpose? If there is a God who is actively involved in our experience, how does this God accomplish his purpose in us? What practical dif-ference does it make for us to believe that there might actually be a God who is actively involved in our experience?

These questions are addressed in what is clearly the best known of all the David stories. This story has even made it to Broadway! One day the headline in the entertainment section of *The New York Times* declared: "Disney Takes on Broadway and the Bible." The Walt Disney Company, which had just invested $34 million to restore the ninety-three-year-old, Ziegfeld-era New Amsterdam Theater, announced that the reopening would be celebrated with a musical ver-sion of the biblical story of King David, composed by Tim Rice and Alan Menken, the team who wrote the music for *Aladdin* and *Beauty and the Beast*. Although the production would cover the whole life of David, the opening sentence of the article read, "Boy Kills Giant with a Single Stone!" New York Mayor Rudy Giuliani summarized what he thought was the lesson of the David story: "It shows young people that fighting against all odds can accomplish things" (*New York Times*, "The Living Arts," August 20, 1996).

Folks who have never read the Bible have heard about David's victory over Goliath. It's such a familiar piece of our cultural heritage that the business section of *Time* magazine could open an article with the words, "The bigger they come, the harder they fall. Such corporate Goliaths as IBM and General Motors once dominated American industry. . . . What happened?" (*Time*, December 28, 1992, p. 28).

You don't even need to believe in God to get what most people assume is the moral of the story: The little guy with a slingshot topples the big guy in the armor. The small and swift succeed where the bulky and slow fail. The bigger they are, the harder they fall. The only problem with that familiar interpretation is that biblically, it isn't the point of the story at all. Just so we wouldn't miss it, the Hebrew storytellers put the lesson of this dramatic tale on the lips of David, just before he whacked Goliath with his stone:

> This very day the LORD will deliver you into my hand . . . *so that* all the earth may know that there is a God in Israel, *and that* all this assembly may know that the LORD does not save by sword and spear; for the battle is the LORD's and he will give you into our hand.
> (1 Samuel 17:46-47, italics added)

The story of David's confrontation with Goliath was told so that the whole earth may know that there is a God who is actively and purposefully at work in human history. It affirms that to the degree to which we allow ourselves to become a part of that divine purpose, God will work in and through us to accomplish God's purpose in God's way through the rough-and-tumble realities of our daily lives. Let's take another look at the dramatic story from that perspective.

The first character on the stage, of course, is Goliath. The text never uses the word *giant*, but it says Goliath's height was "six cubits and a span," which is about ten feet. Goliath is the all-time Alpha male of the Old Testament: bigger than Shaquille O'Neal, stronger than Arnold Schwarzenegger, and badder than "Stone Cold" Steve Austin of the World Wrestling Federation. The text goes to great detail in describing Goliath's armor. This is interesting because recent excavations at Ekron, twenty miles west of Jerusalem, have confirmed that the

Philistines held a monopoly on iron smelting and were highly advanced in the production of swords and shields. No wonder their weapons intimidated the Israelite nomads!

In light of the story's stated purpose, however, the most important thing about Goliath is not his size, nor his weapons, but what he represents. Goliath personifies everything that defies the presence, power, and purpose of God. Goliath represents all those "principalities and powers" that reject the authority of God.

Have you noticed that "giants" never recognize any power higher than themselves? That's just how giants always are; it must be in their genes. Giants of every age and culture, bullies of every political or religious persuasion, Goliaths in every organization or locker room operate on the assumption that there is nothing greater than their own self-interest. They claim absolute authority for themselves and create the impression that everyone and everything else should submit to their control.

If we take the Bible seriously, we can identify some of the God-defying "giants" in our world today. There's the giant of violence, whether it takes the form of war in Bosnia, political turmoil in Africa, the violence of our city streets, or the meanness in our own souls. There's the giant of hunger and poverty, robbing God's children of the basic necessities of life. There's the giant of militarism, fulfilling Dwight Eisenhower's prophetic warning about the "military-industrial complex" that gobbles up the resources of the nations and convinces us that military power is our only source of security. There's the giant of disease, the lack of adequate health care for most of the world's people, the injustice of systems that ensure health care for the rich and sickness for the poor. There's the giant of crass immorality, the perversion, cheapening, and abuse of the good gift of human sexuality. There's the giant of environmental destruction, the selfish abuse of God's creation for short-term profits with no concern for long-term effects.

Closer to home, we face God-defying Goliaths in our own lives: those deeply personal passions and powers within us that contradict the life-giving goodness of God. What man has not faced the giant of consuming greed, the ravenous desire for more and more of everything? What man has not wrestled with the giant of crass selfishness and arrogant pride, the all-consuming passion for everything and everyone to serve our needs? What man has not confronted the giants of self-destructive addictions, devastating defeats, debilitating fears, heart-breaking conflicts, or incomprehensible human pain? And what man has not had to deal with the giant of our passionate need to be in control? In our homes, in our relationships, in our careers, we want to hold the remote control in our hand! We want to exercise autonomous authority over our own lives and those of the people around us.

Another thing giants have in common is that they control by fear. That's where we find Saul. Ironically, Saul had been chosen as king because he was so virile himself. But in this story we find him quivering in fear before the giant (1 Samuel 17:11). Saul and his armies are absolutely immobilized by the defiant arrogance of Goliath. And every guy I know—at least every guy who tells the truth!—has known the paralysis of fear: fear of failure, fear of loss, fear of weakness, fear of getting old, fear of sexual impotence, fear of the future, and perhaps most common of all, the fear of a loss of control.

I was in the mountains of North Carolina in the summer of 1998 when thousands of acres of rural Florida were going up in flame. When the wind drove the fires toward Ormond Beach, I called my friend and fellow pastor Phil Roughton to check up on the safety of his family. At the end of our conversation, Phil said, "It's scary. We all sort of think we have life under control, that we can keep things in order, but this is something we really can't control."

Enter David. He stands out because he is the only actor on the stage who is not frozen with fear. David is the only person who dares to believe that God is actively involved in the drama of life. David takes one good look at Goliath and asks, "Who is this uncircumcised Philistine that he should defy the armies of the living God?" (1 Samuel 17:26). Who is Goliath compared to the power of God?

A millennium later, the apostle Paul asked the same question: "If God is for us, who can be against us?" (Romans 8:31b NIV). Fifteen centuries after that, Martin Luther turned the same theme into the marching hymn of the Reformation:

> Did we in our own strength confide, our striving would be losing,
> were not the right man on our side, the man of God's own choosing.
> . . . .
> The Prince of Darkness grim, we tremble not for him;
> his rage we can endure, for lo, his doom is sure;
> one little word shall fell him.

As a teenager, David brings one of the most inspiring and infuriating gifts of adolescence to the battle: a sense of immeasurable possibilities. But this isn't a gift his elder brothers are ready to receive. They might be shaking in their boots at the presence of Goliath and the Philistine armies, but no one is questioning their fear! Eliab—David's oldest brother, who appeared so strong that Samuel almost anointed him to be king—is angry. He questions David, "Why have you come down here? Who's taking care of the sheep in your absence? I know *you*! You're here just to see the battle, aren't you?" (1 Samuel 17:28, paraphrased). David's response "What have I done *now*?" provides a fascinating picture of sibling relationships in Jesse's family. David was evidently the little brother who was blamed for everything that went wrong. King Saul takes one look at the shepherd from Bethlehem and says what everyone, including David, already knows: "You are not able to go against this Philistine to fight with him; for you are just a boy, and he has been a warrior from his youth" (1 Samuel 17:33).

Of course, Saul is absolutely correct. By all human standards, David is utterly incapable of overcoming Goliath. He is up against a power he cannot defeat alone. That's an important lesson. We don't like to admit that there is anything we can't handle. We hate to concede that the giants might actually be more powerful than we are. It's really tough for us to acknowledge our need of strength beyond our own. But there's no use trying to take on the giants by ourselves. They are bigger and stronger, and they will always win. David, however, remembers the way God saved him from lions and bears who came to attack his sheep. Drawing on that experience of God's power in the past, he claims God's power for the future: "The LORD, who saved me from the paw of the lion and from the paw of the bear, will save me from the hand of this Philistine" (1 Samuel 17:37).

The next scene is pure comic relief. I can picture it as a sketch on *Saturday Night Live*! Saul, who was too afraid to use his armor himself, attempts to put it on David. Who knows? Maybe Saul secretly hoped people would think he had taken on Goliath himself. He tries to make David look like a king, dresses him like a warrior, and equips him with the same weapons Goliath will use. But the king's shield and sword don't fit. In fact, they get in David's way and look downright foolish. It is a comic portrayal of the affirmation that "the LORD does not save by sword and spear" (1 Samuel 17:47). Saul's weapons are not David's weapons, nor are they God's.

When will we ever get it through our skulls (a rather convincing image, considering what happened to Goliath!) that we cannot defeat Goliath with Goliath's weapons? We cannot overcome violence with violence. When we attempt to use evil to destroy evil, we end up increasing the total amount of evil in the world. When will we practice the lesson Martin Luther King, Jr., tried to teach us?

> Violence solves no social problems; it merely creates new and more complicated ones. . . . To retaliate with hate and bitterness would do nothing but intensify the hate in the world. Along the way of life, someone must have sense enough and morality enough to cut off the chain of hate. This can be done only by projecting the ethics of love to the center of our lives.
> ("Nonviolence and Racial Justice," *A Testament of Hope,* San Francisco: Harper & Row, 1986, pp. 7-8)

God's purpose can only be accomplished in God's way with God's power. David lays aside the king's armor. With nothing but his naked trust in God, David picks up his sling—just the way Michelangelo carved him in marble—and walks out onto the stage of human history for the climactic confrontation with the giant. Goliath mocks him, but David uses his size and speed to wear the bulky, slow giant down. Finally, David sees his opportunity. He loads up his sling and lets it fly. The stone hits the giant smack between the eyes. Goliath tumbles to the ground, and the biblical account underscores that "there was no sword in David's hand" (1 Samuel 17:50).

In the end, David uses Goliath's sword to finish off Goliath, which reminds me of Jesus' warning that "all who take the sword will perish by the sword" (Matthew 26:52). With the giant struck down, the Philistines who had placed their trust in him flee. And the story has been told from generation to generation so that all the earth will know (1) that there is a God who is active in human history; (2) that God saves by God's own means; and (3) that ultimately the battle is the Lord's. God will ultimately be victorious over every defiant power.

The dramatic story of David's victory over Goliath is not primarily about the way the small and swift defeat the bulky and slow. Though that does sometimes happen, the brutal reality is that there are just as many times when the big guy rubs the little guy out. This drama is not ultimately about the way a sincere little hero defeats the arrogant bully. Although that does happen, a lot of little heroes end up with a lot of black eyes along the way. Someone told me that the only thing necessary for lions to lie down with lambs is an almost inexhaustible supply of lambs. There's no promise that every little guy will necessarily be victorious in every confrontation with the giants. It's a tough world out there, and just because we are faithful to God doesn't mean we won't get knocked down.

David's victory over Goliath is ultimately about a God who acts in human history through ordinary people who place more confidence in God than they do in themselves, and who are willing to place more trust in God than they do in their human powers. It is ultimately about the way God accomplishes God's purpose through people who refuse to attempt to accomplish a good end by evil means. It is about the way ordinary people allow their faith in God to become the power source to energize them when they face the giants in their lives. David is the star character in this drama because he is the only person on the stage who dares to believe that God will accomplish God's purpose by God's means, and David is the only person who puts himself on the line to prove it.

I'm somewhat frustrated each year when the nation celebrates the life of Martin Luther King, Jr. We generally ignore the fact that Dr. King's commitment to nonviolence and civil rights was deeply rooted in his faith in God. In describing his "Pilgrimage to Nonviolence," he wrote, "I have . . . become more and more convinced of the reality of a personal God." King said there was a time when God was little more than an interesting topic for theological or philosophical debate. But the reality of God's presence in his life had been validated in the everyday pressure and tension of the struggle in which he had been engaged:

> In the midst of outer dangers I have felt an inner calm and known resources of strength that only God could give. In many instances I have felt the power of God transforming the fatigue of despair into the buoyancy of hope. I am convinced that the universe is under the control of a loving purpose and that in the struggle for righteousness man has cosmic companionship. (*Testament of Hope*, p. 40)

The theme of "cosmic companionship" became a common refrain in Martin Luther King's sermons and speeches, often building toward his affirmation that "even though the arc of the moral universe is long, it bends toward justice" ("Love, Law, and Civil Disobedience," *Testament of Hope,* p. 52). His confidence that "the battle is the Lord's" reverberates in one of his often-repeated conclusions, which would bring his congregations to their feet:

> Good Friday may reign for a day, but ultimately it must give way to the triumphant beat of the Easter drums. Evil may so shape events that Caesar will occupy a palace and Christ a cross, but one day that same Christ will rise up and split history into A.D. and B.C., so that even the life of Caesar must be dated by his name. So in Montgomery we can walk and never get weary, because we know that there will be a great camp meeting in the promised land of freedom and justice. ("Nonviolence and Racial Justice," *Testament of Hope,* p. 9)

The witness of Martin Luther King, Jr., cannot be fully explained in terms of political power, any more than David's victory over Goliath can be explained by his accuracy with the sling. King's influence in American history bears witness to a God who is at work to accomplish a redemptive purpose and chooses to do it through people who place their trust in God and who make themselves available to accomplish God's purpose by God's means. That's what it means to live by faith, to live spiritually, to live from the inside out.

But let's face it: Most of our lives will not become the stuff of history. We generally face the giants on a much more ordinary level of existence. The expressions of doctrinal theism and practical atheism show up in the mundane stuff of my life. Although I have always affirmed my faith in God, there have been many times when I have worked as if everything depended on my own human strength, power, wisdom, and talents. I've been to more church meetings than I care to admit that opened and closed with prayer, but at which, between the two prayers, we might as well have been in the boardroom of a bank or around the table of a civic club. In recent years, however, I have been led to a deeper understanding of what it means to actually live out of a life that is centered in faith and shaped by prayer. I am discovering new ways in which God is an active player in the drama of my life. As I have moved to a deeper place of practical trust in God, I have seen God act in amazing ways in my family, in my relationships with others, in the struggles with giants in my own personality, and in the church that I serve.

I have shared this same struggle with others and have seen the way they have experienced the inner calm and personal strength that Dr. King described. I am more convinced than ever before that there is a God who is actively involved in our lives and that to the degree to which we make ourselves available to it, God will use us to accomplish God's own purpose by God's own means in this world.

One of the men who read this manuscript said that the reason many men are "practical atheists" is because no one ever taught them how to put into practice the faith in which they believe. He expressed his frustration when he wrote:

> I have certainly heard that before (all those Sunday mornings have not been completely wasted), and I believe it to be true, and I would like to do something about it, but . . . no one has ever showed me "how." Although as children we dutifully went to church each Sunday morning piled in the family car, we apparently didn't learn that making God a part of your life every day was something we should, could, and wanted to do. Now, you expect us to all of a sudden change that pattern? OK, I'm ready—tell me how, and I don't want to sing in the choir.

How is the living reality of God validated in our daily experience? How do we make ourselves available to the redemptive purpose and loving power of God? The only answer is spiritual discipline. Just the way the discipline of regular physical exercise prepares us to run a race or win a game, the practice of spiritual discipline strengthens us to face the giants when we confront them in our daily lives.

In describing the process of spiritual discipline, John Ortberg makes a very helpful distinction between "trying" and "training." He says that any of us could "try" to run in the Olympics, but the only people who actually make it are the ones who "train" for them. Training—the regular practice of specific disciplines—is what makes the difference. (See *The Life You've Always Wanted*, Grand Rapids: Zondervan, 1997, pp. 45-51.)

I went into training at the downtown YMCA this year. I've been an off-and-on runner for a couple of decades. Across the years, I have water-skied and played a very mediocre game of tennis. But having passed the age of fifty, and having watched a whole lot of guys change physically with age, I decided it was time to get on a regular fitness program. The process I went through at the "Y" led me to create my own process by which we develop the disciplines of spiritual fitness.

1. *Acknowledge that you need help.* I had made some inadequate stabs at exercise programs, but I needed a coach to get me going in the right direction. In terms of spiritual fitness, sometimes the biggest step is the first one. It is the step we take when we acknowledge that we need help and choose to walk through the door of a church, join a men's group, sign up at a Bible study, or call a trusted Christian friend and ask him for his advice.

2. *Find out where you are.* The first thing the folks at the "Y" did was put me through a fitness assessment program. All that stuff about being a skinny seventh-grader really paid off—most middle-aged guys would covet my body-fat percentages! But I needed help on flexibility and muscle tone. So, take a spiritual inventory of your life. What has been your spiritual experience in the past? How's your biblical knowledge? Where have you experienced some sense of God's presence in your life? What do you need or expect to happen as you develop your spiritual fitness?

3. *Commit yourself to a change of lifestyle.* I began putting my hours at the "Y" on my calendar just like any other appointment. I put my money behind it with a membership. I told my wife and a colleague in my office that I wanted them to help me be accountable. In the same sense, spiritual development requires a commitment to a lifestyle change to include time for worship, Bible study, and prayer in your daily pattern. The best resource I've seen is the *Disciple* Bible study, which requires a thirty-four-week commitment to daily Bible reading and a weekly group session.

4. *As Nike taught us, "Just do it!"* Set aside a daily time (15-30 minutes is a good start) for Bible reading and prayer. It doesn't take the discipline of a monk; you just need to make this time a part of the regular pattern of your life. Use a practical, daily devotional guide such as *365 Meditations for Men* (Nashville: Dimensions for Living, 1998). If your congregation follows the lectionary of Bible readings for worship, *The Upper Room Disciplines* will connect your daily devotional time with the scripture lessons you will hear on Sunday morning.

5. *Allow your discipline to influence the rest of your life.* As time went by in my exercise program, I began to see its effects in what I ate, how I walked and sat, and how I slept. It began to influence other areas of my life in practical ways. The point of spiritual discipline is to open our lives to the continuing influence and presence of the Spirit

of God so that our attitudes and actions are shaped in the likeness of Jesus Christ. I noticed that the YMCA trainer who got me started wore a "WWJD" bracelet. Whether we wear it on a bracelet or not, it's the right question: "What would Jesus do?"

6. *Celebrate your strength.* Because so many people from my congregation work downtown, it's a small celebration when we see one another at the downtown "Y." They keep me going and encourage me along the way. In terms of spiritual fitness, it is absolutely essential that we celebrate our personal relationship with Christ in the fellowship of other Christian people through worship. There is no solitary Christianity.

I'm sticking with my fitness program at the "Y." I'll never be a giant, but I fully expect that someday I will need the physical strength it is adding to my body. I don't want to be like the person in the old TV commercial who says, "I've fallen, and I can't get up!" And I'm sticking with my spiritual disciplines so that I will be prepared to face the giants that are sure to come in my life.

> I love you, O LORD, my strength.
> The LORD is my rock, my fortress, and my deliverer,
>   my God, my rock in whom I take refuge,
>   my shield, and the horn of my salvation, my stronghold.
> . . . .
> He delivered me from my strong enemy,
>   and from those who hated me;
>   for they were too mighty for me.
> They confronted me in the day of my calamity;
>   but the LORD was my support.
> . . . .
> For who is God except the LORD?
>   And who is a rock besides our God?—
> the God who girded me with strength,
>   and made my way safe.
>   (Psalm 18:1-2, 17-18, 31-32)

Time Out

F
A
I
T
H

1. *Name your "giants."* Where have you faced Goliath? What giants have defied God's loving, life-giving purpose in your life, your home, your friendships, your work? Name the "principalities and powers" with which you contend. How have you confronted them?

2. *Tell the truth.* In what specific ways have you been a "doctrinal theist and practical atheist"? In other words, in what ways do you profess to believe in God but act as though God does not exist? What difference would it make for the faith you affirm on Sunday to actually influence your life during the week? Give some examples.

3. *Check your weapons.* What will it mean for you to accomplish God's purpose in God's way with God's weapon of *love*? How do you respond to the witness of Martin Luther King, Jr., which is described in this chapter? How can the example of his life influence your own?

4. *Find your pattern.* Walk through the steps I took in getting into the fitness program at the YMCA. Where are you in the process of your own spiritual fitness?

5. *Prayer.* Allow these penetrating questions from Isaac Watts (1674–1748) to guide you into a time of personal reflection on David's story:

F
A
I
T
H

Am I a soldier of the cross,
    a follower of the Lamb,
and shall I fear to own his cause,
    or blush to speak his name?

Must I be carried to the skies
    on flowery beds of ease,
while others fought to win the prize,
    and sailed through bloody seas?

Are there no foes for me to face?
    Must I not stem the flood?
Is this vile world a friend to grace,
    to help me on to God?

Sure I must fight, if I would reign;
    increase my courage, Lord.
I'll bear the toil, endure the pain,
    supported by thy word.

Friendship

You Need a Soul-Friend to Succeed

1 Samuel 18:1-5; 20:12-17

> Were I to describe the blessing I desire in life, I could be
> happy in a few but faithful friends.
>
> —*Meriwether Lewis,* Undaunted Courage

How do you define *success*? It's not too early in our examination of the life of David to ask that question. In the New Revised Standard Version, the word *success* (or a derivative of it) appears four times in 1 Samuel 18.

> David went out and was successful wherever Saul sent him. (1 Samuel 18:5)
> David had success in all his undertakings; for the LORD was with him. (verse 14)
> When Saul saw that [David] had great success, he stood in awe of him. (verse 15)
> David had more success than all the servants of Saul, so that his fame became very great. (verse 30)

How do you measure success? A management consultant told of a Chicago businessman who declared that his company's success was based on three principles:

1. A man has a right to be selfish.
2. A man has a right to keep whatever he earns.
3. A man's life is his own business and nobody else's.

Based on that definition of success, Daddy Warbucks was correct in the Broadway musical *Annie* when he declared that it doesn't matter who you step on while you're on the way to the top if you're not planning to come back down. If that's the kind of success you want, you can probably achieve it without friends. In fact, being friendless is almost a prerequisite!

But how does the Bible define success? What is "success" for a man who is attempting to live from the inside out as a person who is spiritually centered in Christ? The word itself just barely makes it into these passages and never appears in the New Testament, but based on the biblical account of David's life, I'll attempt my own homegrown definition. *Success* is fulfilling the unique purpose of God for your life as a part of the redemptive purpose that God is at work to accomplish in human history. For a Christian, being successful means becoming the whole person God intends for you to be in the light of God's love revealed in Jesus Christ.

A few years ago I went through a very difficult time in the ministry. It was one of those times when everything seemed to be going against me and I wasn't sure that I understood the situation or had a clue as to what I should do about it. Nothing that had made me feel "successful" in the past seemed to be working. In the midst of it, I received a letter from a longtime friend who had seen me at my best and at my worst. He wrote, "I know that the situation is no fun, but if you can relax and just let Jim be Jim, good things will happen—or at least, better peace." He reminded me of the way I often quoted G. K. Chesterton, who said that angels can fly because they take themselves so lightly. By my friend's encouragement, I was reminded that the only thing necessary to be a "success" is to be the person God created, claimed, and calls us to be.

David's success was inextricably bound up with King Saul and with Saul's son Jonathan, the heir-apparent to the throne. In this chapter we will see the way God's purpose was fulfilled through David's friendship with Jonathan. In the next, we will see the way that same purpose was fulfilled in spite of David's conflict with Saul.

Mickey and Donald, Batman and Robin, Lucy and Ethel, Cliff and Norm, Seinfeld and Kramer; none of the famous friendships of our media culture can hold a candle to this: "The soul of Jonathan was bound to the soul of David, and Jonathan loved him as his own soul"

(1 Samuel 18:1). When both of their lives were threatened by Saul, we read that Jonathan "loved [David] as he loved his own life" (1 Samuel 20:17). And after Jonathan died, David sang one of the most eloquent elegies of all time:

> I am distressed for you, my brother Jonathan;
> greatly beloved were you to me;
>   your love to me was wonderful,
> passing the love of women. (2 Samuel 1:26)

Considering what we know of David's wives, his concubines, and his torrid affair with Bathsheba, those words become a downright shocking measure of his love for Jonathan (though I do not find them a convincing basis upon which to read homosexuality into the text).

Jonathan had already established himself as a daring officer in Saul's army, a leader in the nation, a hero to the people. Everyone liked Jonathan, and everyone knew that he would one day be king. Think of the way the world has fallen in love with Prince William, the heir to the British throne. That must be the way people felt about Jonathan. And that is what makes what follows such a dramatic moment:

> Then Jonathan made a covenant with David, because he loved him as his own soul. Jonathan stripped himself of the robe that he was wearing, and gave it to David, and his armor, and even his sword and his bow and his belt. (1 Samuel 18:3-4)

Jonathan gave David the symbols of his birthright, the signs of his leadership, the emblems of his future role as king. Jonathan surrendered what the world would have defined as "success" to participate with God in the divine purpose that was being fulfilled through David. Jonathan's story sets a biblical standard for friendship that goes all the way to the soul. In these chapters from 1 Samuel, we can discover several defining marks of the kind of soul-friendship that can be a part of the fulfillment of God's purpose in our lives.

First, "Jonathan took great delight in David" (1 Samuel 19:1). My guess is that David and Jonathan laughed a lot. Sitting around a feasting table, riding through the fields, resting beside a rushing stream, falling off to sleep out under the stars, they experienced the sheer delight that is a sure sign of soul-level friendship.

The first defining mark of soul-friendship is this: *It is a sheer delight to be with soul-friends.* My soul-friends make me smile when I hear their voices on the phone. We laugh a lot. Mark Twain said that "to get the full value of a joy you must have somebody to divide it with" (*Context*, August 15, 1988, p. 6). Soul-friends multiply the joy of life.

In my book *Men at Midlife* (Nashville: Dimensions for Living, 1993), I described my group of clergy cronies as "ruthlessly honest, laughter-addicted, faith-stretching soul-brothers who, like Chaucer's pilgrims on the way to Canterbury, tell their tales in a winter solstice retreat" (p. 9). The group has been together for sixteen years now. We recently realized that we were heading into the next passage of male identity when one of us became the first to experience the marriage of a child. Because I'm the oldest in the group, I can even confess that some of us are starting to think about retirement! As the years go by, many things about our times together have changed, but one element that remains the same is the laughter. It's the kind of laughter that was described in a wonderful way by theologian Reinhold Niebuhr, who would not be remembered by most seminary students for his sense of humor.

> Laughter is our reaction to immediate incongruities. . . . Humor is, in fact, a prelude to faith; and laughter is the beginning of prayer. In the holy of holies, laughter is swallowed up in prayer and humor is fulfilled by faith. (*Context*, April 15, 1992; p. 5)

When Sam Keen diagnosed the most common spiritual ailment of men today, he said it is not "our lust for power, our insatiable hunger for gadgets, or our habit of repressing women and the poor." Rather, he said, it is our lack of joy. "Most of the men I know are decent, serious, and hard-working, and would like to make the world a better place. What they are not is juicy, sensual, and fun" (*Fire in the Belly*, New York: Bantam, 1991, p. 171). Keen's diagnosis is absolutely accurate for most of the men I know. It was confirmed by one of the brothers who read the first draft of this book and said, "Even if we feel joy, we have been conditioned that 'manliness' requires stoicism and seriousness, except for our spouses and girlfriends, where we are supposed to provide a laugh a minute!" What's missing for many men is joy. They are *deadly* serious. This would be true for me except for soul-friends who are "juicy, sensual, and fun." I know that God's purpose in my life has been energized and enriched through them.

The second defining mark of soul-friendship is this: *Soul-friendship is faithful.* First Samuel 20:14 records words spoken to David by Jonathan: "If I am still alive, show me the faithful love of the LORD; but if I die, never cut off your faithful love from my house."

"If I am still alive" was no rhetorical statement. Their lives were very much up for grabs. Jonathan's loyalty to David put him in direct opposition to Saul, who tried to pin both of them to the wall with his spear (1 Samuel 18:10-11; 20:33-34). Fortunately, Saul wasn't a very good shot, but there was every possibility that he might not miss the next time! With that kind of threat from his father, it was no small thing for Jonathan to describe his faithfulness to David as an expression of "the faithful love of the LORD."

Soul-friendship is faithful. It hangs in there for the long haul, regardless of the odds stacked against it. It holds on through the best and the worst that life can bring. I caught a glimpse of that kind of friendship on a rainy day in Bath, England. I was wandering around the Cathedral, waiting for the rain to stop, when I started reading the memorial stones. This was my favorite.

William Clarke Jervoise, Esq.
A Captain in the British Navy
Who Departed this Life Dec. 6th 1837
Aged 48
Abounding In All Those Qualities
Which Constitute A Christian and a Gentlemen

Kind, Affectionate and Generous.
Friendship With Him
Was More Than A Name;
It Was A Tie That He Hallowed,
A Band He Never Broke.

Jonathan never broke his band of friendship with David. He defended David before his father. He conspired with David for David's escape. He protected David from death. Though the biblical text doesn't record it, my guess is that he thought of David with his dying breath.

One of the all-time great friendships in American history was between Meriwether Lewis and William Clark. The story of their heroic leadership of the Corps of Discovery came alive for me through Ken Burns' PBS television series and the Stephen Ambrose best-seller entitled *Undaunted Courage: Meriwether Lewis, Thomas Jefferson, and the Opening of the American West* (New York: Simon and Schuster, 1996). Responding to Lewis's invitation to join in the expedition, Clark wrote:

> I will chearfully join you . . . and partake of the dangers, difficulties, and fatigues, and I anticipate the honors & rewards of the result of such an enterprise. . . . This is an undertaking fraited with many difeculties, but My friend I do assure you that no man lives with whome I would perfur to undertake Such a Trip &c. as yourself. . . . My friend, I join you with hand & Heart.

Lewis replied with the same bond of friendship for Clark:

> I could neither hope, wish, or expect from a union with any man on earth, more perfect support or further aid in the discharge of the several duties of my mission, than that, which I am confident I shall derive from being associated with yourself. (*Undaunted Courage*, p. 104, with spelling and punctuation from the original text)

Lewis and Clark's friendship enabled them to accomplish a mission neither of them could have accomplished alone. Lewis's life ended in a Shakespearean tragedy of depression, alcohol, and suicide. But even as he drifted in and out of his depression, the people around him reported that he said he was confident that Clark had heard of his distress and was on his way to help. When everything else failed him, he remembered the faithfulness of his friend. That's the kind of soul-friendship that becomes a human expression of "the faithful love of the Lord."

The third defining mark of soul-friendship is this: *Soul-friendship is something you feel.* We see the emotional power of it in David's story when David's conflict with Saul becomes so severe that David has to escape, leaving Jonathan behind.

> David rose from beside the stone heap and prostrated himself with his face to the ground. He bowed three times, and they kissed each other, and wept with each other; David wept the more. Then Jonathan said to

David, "Go in peace, since both of us have sworn in the name of the
LORD, saying, 'The Lord shall be between me and you, and between my
descendants and your descendants, forever.' " (1 Samuel 20:41-42)

Does the emotion in that scene make you just a little uncomfortable? Does that kind of kissing, hugging, and slobbering all over each
other seem just a little strange? The fact is that most men in our culture are, to varying degrees, homophobic. We are afraid of close relationships with other men because it is so difficult for us to imagine a
warm, intimate relationship that does not lead to sexual intercourse. I
come from solid German stock. I may have hugged and kissed my
father when I was a little boy, but by the time my glands were exploding as a teenager, I had learned to shake his hand and keep a
respectable distance, the way real men are supposed to do. I'm not
sure that after childhood I ever kissed him, and I'm quite sure he never
kissed me. But just look at the way the French and Italians slobber all
over one another! Maybe it was because of the cold weather in central
Europe, but for some reason, my forebears passed on a genetic tendency to relational frigidity. By God's grace, I've gotten over it and
have discovered the strength and joy that comes from a brotherly hug.

For the most part, men in our culture are conditioned from childhood to hide their deepest emotions. I was leaving a small-town movie
theater in the mountains of North Carolina when I overheard part of
a conversation between an elementary-school-age girl and her mother.
My guess is that the younger brother beside her had made fun of her
for crying at the end of the movie. She poked him in the arm as she
asked her mother, "Why don't boys cry?" I sometimes wonder how
much of the emotional and physical dis-ease we see in men today
could be avoided or healed with the gift of a soul-friend with whom we
were allowed to cry.

The evidence in the story of David and Jonathan is that soul-friendship is something you *feel*; it goes to your guts. Soul-friendship gives a
man the freedom to share his deepest hurt, his most bitter pain, his
greatest sorrow. Soul-friends let their feelings flow.

John Wesley, the founder of the Methodist movement, may have
been a rather cerebral man, but his brother Charles seems like the
kind of person who would hang around with the guys after they had
bound their souls together in prayer. You can feel the passion of his
friendships in one of his lesser-known hymns.

If death my friend and me divide,
thou dost not, Lord, my sorrow chide,
or frown my tears to see;
restrained from passionate excess,
thou bidst me mourn in calm distress
for them that rest in thee.

I feel a strong immortal hope,
which bears my mournful spirit up
beneath its mountain load;
redeemed from death, and grief, and pain,
I soon shall find my friend again
within the arms of God.

Pass a few fleeting moments more
and death the blessing shall restore
which death has snatched away;
for me thou wilt the summons send,
and give me back my parted friend
in that eternal day.

I included those words in a note to Dan Johnson to celebrate our thirty years of friendship. I told him that if he went to heaven before me, I would feel what Wesley described. Dan responded by pointing out a reference note about another Wesley hymn, "Come, O Thou Traveler Unknown."

Dear Jim,

Thanks for your love and your friendship. . . . [I]t has been a very good 30 years together. I also thought of "Come, O Thou Traveler Unknown" and the note that says John Wesley tried to teach the hymn at Bolton two weeks after his brother's death, but broke down when he came to the lines "my company before is gone, and I am left alone with thee." If, by God's providence, you should pass over before I do, I shall surely never be able to sing that hymn, for you have been my dearest friend and more. But in the meantime, I shall resort to ongoing harassment and jibes, interspersed with an abundance of laughter and hilarity . . . !

An unimpeachable sign of soul-friendship is the freedom to share our honest feelings with each other!

The fourth and final defining mark of soul-friendship from the story of David and Jonathan is this: *Soul-friendship looks to the future.* The scene recorded in 1 Samuel 23:16-18 looks toward the fulfillment of God's purpose in David's life:

> Jonathan set out and came to David at Horesh; there he strengthened his hand through the LORD. He said to him, "Do not be afraid; for the hand of my father Saul shall not find you; you shall be king over Israel, and I shall be second to you; my father Saul also knows that this is so." Then the two of them made a covenant before the LORD.

Jonathan could see and accept what Saul denied, namely, that God had chosen David to be the future king. Jonathan's calling was to strengthen the fulfillment of God's purpose in David's life. Soul-friends always look to the future, to the fulfillment of God's good purpose in each other's lives. They strengthen each other to accomplish God's best for each other.

When Henry David Thoreau went to Walden, his neighbors helped him "raise," or build, his house. Thoreau wrote of his new friends, "No man was ever more honored in the character of his raisers than I. They are destined, I trust, to assist at the raising of loftier structures one day" (*Walden,* Economy). No man was ever more honored in his "raisers" than David was by his friendship with Jonathan. Through Jonathan's friendship, David was strengthened to fulfill God's calling in his life. Jonathan gave up what the world would have called success in order to fulfill that unique calling of God in David's life.

In the same way, Thomas Merton described the way God brought half a dozen other skeptical, searching, struggling students at Columbia University into his life "and made us friends, in such a way that our friendship would work powerfully to rescue us from the confusion and the misery in which we had come to find ourselves." Looking back after he had come to faith in Christ, he could see how through their sharing of ideas along with their "fears and difficulties and desires and hangovers," they "were bound together and fused and vitalized and prepared for the action of grace" (*A Thomas Merton Reader,* New York: Image Books, 1989, p. 87). Those friendships were an essential part of the fulfillment of God's purpose in and through Merton's life. He became one of the most influential interpreters of the spiritual life in this century.

In the fall of 1992, I found myself in the coronary care unit of St. Joseph's Hospital with what was diagnosed as cardiomyopathy, a virus-like condition that weakens the muscles of the heart. The cardiologist said the only medical cure was a heart transplant, but because we had found it in the early stages, we would attack it with steroids. Word of my condition spread through the United Methodist connection to friends and colleagues around the world. (At one point I felt like Mark Twain, who, when the newspaper mistakenly reported his death, said that the rumors of his demise were greatly exaggerated!) Through it all, I felt the healing power of the love and prayers of all my friends and colleagues. When the ordeal was behind me and my heart was back to normal, I thanked the cardiologist for saving my life. He replied, "You'd better thank all those folks who prayed for you, because I'm not sure that anything we did made much difference." I know what it means to be strengthened by the friendship and prayers of my friends.

God's purpose in David's life was fulfilled, in large measure, because of his friendship with Jonathan. In the same way, Christ-centered soul-friendship enables us to become the whole, complete person God intends for us to be. It is a strengthening gift through which the Spirit accomplishes God's good purpose in our lives—not to mention that it's a whole lot of fun, too!

> How very good and pleasant it is
>   when kindred live together in unity!
> It is like the precious oil on the head,
>   running down upon the beard,
> on the beard of Aaron,
>   running down over the collar of his robes.
> It is like the dew of Hermon,
>   which falls on the mountains of Zion.
> For there the LORD ordained his blessing,
>   life forevermore.
>
> (Psalm 133)

Time Out

1. *Take stock of your friendships.* Eleanor Roosevelt wrote, "I made the discovery long ago that very few people made a great difference to me, but that those few mattered enormously. I live surrounded by people, and my thoughts are always with the few that matter whether they are near or far" (*No Ordinary Time,* p. 453). Who are the people who matter most to you? Name them. List some of the ways God has used them to influence your life and faith.

2. *Have you found a soul-friend like Jonathan?* Have you found a soul-friend whom you can delight in; one who is faithful; one with whom you can share your deepest feelings? Have you found a brother who can see God's purpose in your life and strengthen you to fulfill it? Have you expressed your gratitude to that person for this gift?

3. *Are you a soul-friend?* How are you at building the kind of soul-friendship David and Jonathan shared? What keeps you from entering into that kind of relationship? What influences from your past prevent the kind of soul-sharing described here?

4. *Listen to Jesus.* Gathered around the table with his disciples on the night before he died, Jesus said, "This is my commandment, that you love one another as I have loved you. . . . You are my friends if you do what I command you. I do not call you servants any longer, . . . but I have called you friends. . . . I am giving you these commands so that you may love one another" (John 15:12-17). What

F
R
I
E
N
D
S
H
I
P

does it mean for you to be a friend of Jesus? How does his friendship with you shape your friendship with others?

5. *Prayer.* This prayer from Charles Wesley (1707–1788) combines our love for Christ and our love for our friends into a life-transforming experience of the love of God. Pray this prayer together in a group or reflect silently upon it.

> Jesus, united by thy grace
> and each to each endeared,
> with confidence we seek thy face
> and know our prayer is heard.
>
> Help us to help each other, Lord,
> each other's cross to bear;
> let all their friendly aid afford,
> and feel each other's care.
> . . . .
> Touched by the lodestone of thy love,
> let all our hearts agree,
> and ever toward each other move,
> and ever move toward thee.
>
> To thee, inseparably joined,
> let all our spirits cleave;
> O may we all the loving mind
> that was in thee receive.

Chapter Five

Surrender

Fighting with Your Future

1 Samuel 18:6-16

> There is a tide in the affairs of men,
> Which, taken at the flood, leads on to fortune;
> Omitted, all the voyage of their life
> Is bound in shallows and in miseries.
>
> —*William Shakespeare*, Julius Caesar *IV, iii*

I knew a guy who was at the top of his profession when he was diagnosed with a progressively debilitating disease. His staff and friends tried to help, but his ability to receive their assistance decreased in direct proportion to the increase in his physical limitations. Offers of assistance were met with hostile resistance. Unable to win the battle over his illness, this man seemed to be in conflict with the people closest to him. He isolated himself and was forced to give up his career earlier than might otherwise have been necessary. I'd say he was fighting with his future.

King Saul was a lot like that man. He is one of the most complex, tragic, and fascinating personalities in the entire Bible. Holocaust scholar Elie Wiesel described Saul as "both pathetic and mysterious . . . profoundly human—even in his failures. . . . More complex than David, more tormented and tortured, Saul lifts us to mountain heights and then drops us into the abyss" (*Five Biblical Portraits,* Notre Dame: University of Notre Dame Press, 1981, pp. 73-74).

The friendship between David and Saul began with the healing songs the young David played to soothe the king's troubled soul. According to the text, "Saul loved [David] greatly" (1 Samuel 16:21). My guess is that Saul always loved David, even when fear had turned his love into hate. It's like that, you know. I've learned the hard way to watch out for the folks who seem to "love" me too greatly or praise me too highly. There is every possibility that their "love" will turn to hate when I fail to live up to all of their expectations.

Tucked away in that back room of my personality with the painful memory of seventh-grade gym class is an equally painful memory of my early years of ministry and a church member who became my biggest fan. Because I was too naive to know any better, I got hooked on the near-adulation this personal cheerleader poured on me. I placed my cheerleader in a role of leadership and influence in the church. Then one day I made a decision that did not fit with this person's expectations. Suddenly, all of the energy that had gone into singing my praises was redirected into a frontal attack on my leadership and integrity. I learned how quickly unhealthy admiration can dissolve into hate.

Like their friendship, the conflict between David and King Saul began with a song as well. It was actually just a little ditty that was sung to the rhythm of banging tambourines as the army marched back from whopping up on the Philistines. It doesn't sound like much of a song to me, but maybe it lost something in the translation. It must have had a better ring in Hebrew. The chorus went, "Saul has killed his thousands, and David his ten thousands." The difference in body counts made Saul furious, and he "eyed David from that day on" (1 Samuel 18:7-9).

On one level, what we have here is a simple drama of male pride, that lusty, competitive spirit that seems to be born into us. There is, of course, a healthy, productive side to all this. It can be a driving force in our desire to be the best we can be. But from peeing contests in childhood and "scoring" by sexual conquests in adolescence, within the multitude of ways adult men measure their manhood in comparison to others, to the wars men lead their nations to fight, we inherit a destructive side to that pride and competitive spirit as well. Many of us are driven by an unspoken fear that another man might make more money, get a better promotion, attract more beautiful women, or drive a hotter car or longer golf ball than we do. We are tempted to do almost anything to protect our prestige and are willing to destroy anyone who appears to be a threat to our power.

But there is more to the tension between David and Saul than jealous pride. *God* is involved here. From the biblical perspective, it was God's intention for David to become king. Everything in the story is measured by the degree to which it works for or against the fulfillment of that divine purpose. Looking back from this perspective, we can see the tide flowing in the affairs of these men. It's all perfectly clear from here. Hindsight is always 20/20, as they say. David and Saul, however, were caught in the immediate flow of events. They could not see the story from the long perspective of history and had to figure it out along the way.

The fact is that our life would be a whole lot easier (though probably a lot less fun!) if we could see it from the perspective from which we read the story of David and Saul. But like them, we are caught up in the immediate events of our time and must discover God's purpose for us in the rough-and-tumble realities of our ordinary lives. We all have good reason to feel a lot like Indiana Jones in *Raiders of the Lost Ark*. When someone asked what he planned to do to get out of the current impossible situation in which he found himself, he replied, "How should I know? I'm making this up as I go along!"

Old Testament scholar Walter Brueggemann defines the conflict in this story as a "contest between the relentless will of [God] and the diseased but powerful will of Saul" (*Interpretation: First and Second Samuel*, Louisville: John Knox Press, 1990, p. 141). His words not only capture the tension in Saul's life but also define the ultimate source of the tension in *our* lives as well. We too are caught in the tension between the relentless, loving, redemptive will of God and the sin-poisoned, though still powerful, will within us. Let's begin with that "relentless will of God."

From Genesis to Revelation, from its table of contents to its supplementary maps, the Bible is absolutely sure that the God who created this earth is determined to save, redeem, heal, and restore it. God will do whatever it takes to accomplish that saving purpose, even if it takes going to the cross.

Jesus called that redemptive purpose the "Kingdom of God," or the "reign" or "rule" of God. Jesus said that he came to bring God's loving rule near, to show us the redemptive reign of God in human terms. It's already here, he said, like a mustard seed growing into a tree. Like leaven in a loaf of bread, it influences everything around it. Jesus taught us to pray that God's Kingdom will come and God's will will be done on earth, just the way it is already fulfilled in heaven. He told his followers to seek the Kingdom first, above and beyond everything else. He promised that if we do that, everything else will be ours as well.

Get the right authority on the throne, and the rest of life will begin to fall into place. Align our life with the reign of God, and it will fulfill the harmony and wholeness that God intended for it. Reject that relentless, loving will of God, and we will end up going against the grain of God's creative design within us. In the end, we will become like Saul, in conflict with ourselves, with God, and with others. Spiritual discipline is the means by which we align the innermost part of our being with that relentless love of God.

I have experienced the human expression of that relentless love of God in parents who have willed only the best for their children. I don't mean manipulative parents who have a neurotic need to relive their lives through their kids. I mean healthy parents whose deepest desire is that their children become the whole persons God created them to be. I've seen their children rebel against that loving purpose, reject their parents' values, deny their parents' guidance or concern. And I've heard those parents say to their kids, "Whatever you do, wherever you go, whatever the consequences of the choices you make, the one thing you cannot do is make me stop loving you." That's a finite, human expression of the infinite, loving will of God.

But there is conflict in this world and in our souls. This conflict is what Brueggemann referred to as the contest between the relentless will of God and "the diseased but powerful will" that is within each of us, just as it was at work within Saul. Any serious consideration of spirituality must face up to this tension.

It should be obvious that not everything that happens in this world is a part of the fulfillment of the purpose of God. Not everything that happens in this world is in accord with God's gracious will. Not everything is an expression of God's Kingdom coming into being on earth the way it is already fulfilled in heaven. Like Saul fighting against God's future in David, there is something within us and within our world that fights against the redemptive reign of God. There is a part of us that asks, with Saul, "What does he want now—my kingdom?" (see 1 Samuel 18:8).

Later in the story the answer to Saul's question becomes ominously clear. Saul tells Jonathan, "As long as the son of Jesse lives upon the earth, neither you nor your kingdom shall be established" (1 Samuel 20:31). For God's purpose to be fulfilled through David, the reign of Saul through Jonathan would have to come to an end. For God's will to be done in our lives, our petty, personal reign must cease. If there is a God who is active in this world, then there is no room in this world for me to be god. It's a little like the early days of *Saturday Night Live,* when Chevy Chase would introduce himself by declaring, "I'm Chevy Chase, and you're not." The Bible tells me that if God is God, then I am not. The answer to Saul's question is simply, Yes, God wants your kingdom, and God wants it *now!*

Maxwell Anderson wrote a biblical play in which two men are debating how to respond to the coming of the Messiah. One man says, "Suppose he's planted like an acorn in a jar, which grows and spreads his roots and must become a tree if he's to live. And then suppose that we're the pottery that hems him in and must be shattered when his swelling roots reach out for earth."

The man's friend replies, "We cannot let self-interest affect us in such a matter. Who values the clay pot if by its breaking this eternal oak is set in our soil to flourish forever?"

With penetrating honesty, the first man responds, "I value my clay pot" ("Journey to Jerusalem," in *The Story of Jesus in the World's Literature,* New York: Creative Age Press, 1946, p. 90).

And so do I. And so do you. Something within us wants to protect our clay pots. Our diseased but powerful will rebels against the loving rule of God. Like Saul, we are caught in the tension between the relentless, loving will of God and the sin-poisoned, though powerful, will that is at work within us. We know in our own experience the soul-struggle the apostle Paul described in dramatic terms:

> I do not understand my own actions. For I do not do what I want, but I do the very thing I hate. . . . For I do not do the good I want, but the evil I do not want is what I do. . . . When I want to do what is good, evil lies close at hand. For I delight in the law of God in my inmost self, but I see in my members another law at war with the law of my mind, making me captive to the law of sin that dwells in my members. (Romans 7:15-23)

I heard that same struggle in the words of a man who, because of his growing faith in Christ, decided to end his relationship with a married woman. Here's how he described his struggle to me:

> I am going through some of the hardest times of my life at the moment. These times are showing me there is no happiness in anything earthly.

I have everything most people ask for and I am no happier than when I had nothing. We have decided not to see each other. It is the hardest thing I have ever been through. We know it is the right thing, though, and that God will reward us in the end. I find it hard to find faith and I am lonely even while around my friends. I simply don't know what to do—so I pray. She is praying that God will save their marriage. While this is hard for me I pray for these things also—and this is the thing that is tearing me apart and testing my faith. I seem to want two opposing things—God in my life and her by my side. I am afraid that I will lose my momentum and fall back to my old ways. I need Christians (especially struggling ones) in my life and a Christian companion that I can be close to. These are the things that I find separate me from the world.

The long, torturous struggle is played out with David fleeing the angry king and Saul in hot pursuit. The more David succeeds, the more violent Saul becomes, confirming the psychological observation that violence is an external expression of frustrated and often unconscious feelings of impotence. The homiletical version of that principle was the legendary note that the preacher had written in the margin of his sermon manuscript that read, "Point very weak here. Yell like hell!"

As a witness of his loyalty to Saul, David spared the king's life in a scene that is as comic as it is deadly (1 Samuel 24:1-22). The New Revised Standard Version gets it right: "Saul went in to relieve himself." The future dangled in the balance while Saul was "relieving himself" (verse 3). David sneaked up behind him and cut off the end of Saul's robe to prove that he had been there. When David revealed his presence to Saul, and Saul realized how close to death he had come, Saul acknowledged the future he did not want to accept: "Now I know that you shall surely be king, and that the kingdom of Israel shall be established in your hand" (1 Samuel 24:20). After David passed up another opportunity to take Saul's life (1 Samuel 26), the king surrendered to the ultimate reality of God's purpose when he cried, "I have been a fool, and have made a great mistake. . . . Blessed be you, my son David! You will do many things and will succeed in them" (1 Samuel 26:21, 25).

The rest is history. We watch in awe-stricken anguish as Saul plays out the tragic drama to its bloody conclusion, finally falling on his own sword (1 Samuel 31:1-7). Sam Keen captured the tragedy of Saul's life and ours when he wrote:

The problem of manhood and the consequent tragedy of history, from the Judeo-Christian perspective, is that men . . . act out the drama of their lives before the audience of their contemporaries rather than before the all-knowing and merciful eye of God. They get mired in the limited perspective of their immediate desire rather than seek harmony with the will of God. (*Fire In the Belly*, New York: Bantam, 1991, p. 102)

If you're like me, you probably need to read that paragraph again. The truth about your life and mine is that we tend to get mired in our own immediate desires and miss out on the harmony we could find in surrender to the loving, life-giving, redemptive will of God. We will never find the fullness of life by defending our own little reign. We will find the fullness of life when we surrender ourselves to the relentless, loving purpose of God that has been revealed to us in Jesus Christ. The early Christians affirmed this kind of surrender when they identified Jesus as "Lord." The Greek word means "one with undisputed ownership or control." They were affirming their personal surrender to the controlling influence of the love of God in Jesus Christ. They had experienced an abdication of personal control in surrender to the power of divine love, but in that abdication, they had discovered abundant life.

The Bible is sure about what the future will hold. The saving purpose of God will ultimately be fulfilled in this creation. The prophet Isaiah envisioned it:

> They shall beat their swords into plowshares,
>   and their spears into pruning hooks;
> nation shall not lift up sword against nation,
>   neither shall they learn war any more.
> (Isaiah 2:4)

Paul saw it beyond the walls of his prison cell:

> Every knee should bend,
>   in heaven and on earth and under the earth,
> and every tongue should confess
>   that Jesus Christ is Lord. (Philippians 2:10-11)

Exiled on Patmos, John anticipated it in spite of the immediate persecution of the Christians by Rome. He spoke it as if the promise had already been fulfilled:

"The kingdom of the world has become the kingdom of our Lord and
of his Messiah,
and he will reign forever and ever." (Revelation 11:15)

We can see the future. Ultimately, God's Kingdom will come, and
God's will shall be done on earth, even as it is already done in heaven.
The relentless will of God's infinite love will be accomplished in human
history. The question this story forces upon us is whether we will choose
to participate in its coming. Will we be like Jonathan, who bound himself to David and gave up his own reign to be a part of God's future? Or
will we be like Saul, who foolishly fought to hold on to his own reign to
the very end? Will we allow our lives, our values, our convictions, our
calling to become a present expression of God's coming reign, or will we
continue fighting with God's future? Will we allow the love of God to be
the controlling power in our personality? Will we allow Jesus Christ,
who will reign as Lord of history, to, become the Lord of our lives?

Franklin Graham is Billy Graham's only son. When he was born, he
was immediately identified as the heir apparent to his father's ministry.
One woman wrote that she hoped Franklin would become a Catholic
so he could be a future Pope. David Van Biema said of Franklin
Graham, "There have been times when the divine plan for him was
hard to divine" (*Time,* May 13, 1996, p. 67). In soulfully sensitive
words, the writer described the conflict Franklin Graham faced.

> The son, almost as soon as he was able, began denying his legacy, turning
> primogeniture into prodigality, forgoing the joys of the spirit for . . .
> alcohol and tobacco, motorcycles and rock 'n' roll. He fought so hard
> against being Billy's kid that he became a sort of Billy the Kid. It would
> be years before his flight from God, fueled by a fear that God would not
> accept his foibles, gave way to the fear of the emptiness without Him. (p.
> 68)

You don't need to be the son of an evangelist to identify with that
description of the way most of us struggle to define the divine plan for
our lives. As I listen to men talk about their own spiritual conflicts, I
hear them saying the same things Franklin Graham said about himself:
"I was afraid if I surrendered my life to Christ I'd have, like, spiritual
handcuffs on me. I had this picture of this God in heaven. . . [who
would] just wait for me to go to the left or right and clobber me."

At the same time, Graham yearned: "Something was missing. . . . There wasn't that joy; there wasn't that fulfillment" (p. 69). Franklin Graham's words sounded familiar to me. I had just read an e-mail message in which a businessman described the reason most of his friends won't go near a church:

> A lot of "guys" aren't in church because church is where they were told as children and young adults to "do this and don't do that," that they had to live up to the highest of all expectations (and that it can't be done), and that God is keeping score. Now you expect them to show up in church to seek and find comfort, guidance and peace of mind??? I don't think so. Your challenge is to show why and how your church is a special place for "guys" to find what they are seeking.

On Franklin Graham's twenty-second birthday, his father confronted him: "You can't continue to play the middle ground. Either you're going to choose to follow and obey [God] or reject him." Those words stuck with Franklin. Some time later, alone in a hotel room, he read Romans 8:1: "There is therefore now no condemnation for those who are in Christ Jesus." Graham realized there was no God with a stick waiting to clobber him. He said, "I put my cigarette out and got down on my knees. . . . I was his. . . . The rebel had found the cause" (p. 69). Instead of fighting against God's future, he found it!

And so can *we*.

> Do not fret because of the wicked;
>   do not be envious of wrongdoers,
> for they will soon fade like the grass,
>   and wither like the green herb.
>
> Trust in the LORD, and do good;
>   so you will live in the land, and enjoy security.
> Take delight in the LORD,
>   and he will give you the desires of your heart.
>
> Commit your way to the LORD;
>   trust in him, and he will act.
> (Psalm 37:1-5)

Time Out

S
U
R
R
E
N
D
E
R

1. *Relationships can be difficult.* When have you experienced conflict similar to the conflict between Saul and David? How did you feel? What was the cause? How did you deal with it?

2. *The relentless will of God.* What is your understanding of the Kingdom (reign, rule) of God? What does it mean for you to seek first the Kingdom of God? What does it mean for you to pray that God's Kingdom will come and God's will be done on earth as it is already fulfilled in heaven? How have you experienced, sensed, felt, or known the relentless, loving purpose of God at work in your life?

3. *The kingdom within.* Dallas Willard writes, "Our 'kingdom' is simply *the range of our effective will.* Whatever we genuinely have the say over is *in* our kingdom. And our having the say over something is precisely what places it within our kingdom" (*The Divine Conspiracy,* HarperSanFrancisco, 1988, p. 21, italics his). To put it in Walter Bruggemann's terms, how do you experience the tension between the relentless will (Kingdom, reign, rule) of God and "the diseased but powerful will" (Kingdom, reign, rule) within us?

4. *The great surrender.* E. Stanley Jones wrote:

The difference between the emphasis on self-realization or on self-surrender seems to be this: in self-realization you try to realize your self, for all the answers are in you. In self-surrender you surrender your self to Jesus Christ, for all the answers are in Him. One leaves you centered

S U R R E N D E R

on you—a self-centered and self-preoccupied person, albeit a religious person. The other loses his self and finds it. For self-realization only comes through self-surrender. You realize your self when you realize Him, and you realize your self when you surrender to Him. (*Victory Through Surrender,* Nashville: Abingdon Press, 1966, p. 8)

Are you ready to realize your life in Christ through surrender to him? What specific changes would this surrender make in your life?

5. *Prayer.* Dag Hammarskjöld described his experience of self-surrender in these words. How do they speak to your inward journey?

I don't know Who—or what—put the question, I don't know when it was put. I don't even remember answering. But at some moment I did answer *Yes* to Someone—or Something—and from that hour I was certain that existence is meaningful and that, therefore, my life, in self-surrender, had a goal. (*Markings,* New York: Knopf, 1964, p. 205)

Charles Wesley offered this invitation to each of us:

His love is mighty to compel;
His conquering love consent to feel,
Yield to his love's resistless power,
And fight against your God no more.
(from "Come, Sinners, to the Gospel Feast")

Sorrow

Where Have All the Flowers Gone?

2 Samuel 1:1-27; 18:24-33

Since boys are taught not to cry, men must learn to weep. . . .
The path to a manly heart runs through the valley of tears.

—*Sam Keen*, Fire in the Belly

There's a guy in my congregation who knows the stats for every baseball team in the Major Leagues. Any time I quote Shakespeare, he reminds me that the Bard's fan club is about the same size as the crowd who expect the Pittsburgh Pirates to win the World Series. In spite of his warning, I can't resist quoting from *King Lear.* The play ends with bloody bodies all over the stage and broken hearts throughout the theater. In the closing speech we hear

> The weight of this sad time we must obey;
> Speak what we feel, not what we ought to say.

I suspect that the fan club for lovers of opera is even smaller than the one for Shakespeare. All I know about opera is that it ain't over until a certain female soloist sings, but a review in *Time* magazine gave me a sense of what it is about. It said that "opera is performed at peak volume" because it deals with matters of passion and power, life and death. The feelings are so large and deep that they cannot be spoken, but "must be sung, shouted, thundered, wept—and shown, in all their delirious force" (*Time,* May 2, 1988, p. 79). I have no illusion that this book will be read by a bunch of opera-singing Shakespeare-lovers, but those two images capture the emotional power of the sorrow in David's life, and they speak to the sorrow in mine.

Like your life and mine, David's life had triumphant moments of soul-tingling success, rib-tickling happiness, and ecstatically erotic passion. There were divine moments when God's presence was as clear as the Florida sun on a cloudless day. But like your life and mine, David's life also had moments of heartbreaking sorrow and painful loss. We may avoid or deny them, but sooner or later, "the weight of this sad time we must obey." There are moments in every man's life when the feelings are so big and deep that they must be thundered and wept in all their delirious force.

Let me tell you about my friend John Brownlee. He was one of the most fully alive men I've ever known. All of his senses were constantly on alert to receive whatever the world had to give. He traveled around the world to hire the first employees for Walt Disney World's Epcot Center. Every trip was punctuated by his discovery of a quaint little restaurant in France, a desert oasis in Morocco, or another London performance of *Starlight Express*.

John was alive to laughter—the kind of laughter that percolates just beneath the surface of life, ready to break through at almost any moment. His infectious smile held within it the innocence of a small boy who never quite grew up or, perhaps, a man who grew up knowing that it was okay to still be a boy.

He had a devilish sense of humor. One day a neighbor who was having no success selling a house came home to find a message on the answering machine. A voice with a heavy Middle Eastern accent said, "I am here from Saudi Arabia only a few days but desire to purchase your house. I will pay cash, but must do so within the next twenty-four hours. Please call me at . . ." Click! The message ended. There was no way to return the call. The frustrated homeowner had told the story all around the neighborhood before John confessed that the voice was his!

John was alive to love—the kind of love that could not but create new life, not once, but four times. His fourth son was conceived after the doctors had declared John's fate, almost as a loving protest against the curse of cancer. John had a lusty, healthy sexuality that made all of us glad to have been created male and female. He drew other men into a depth of friendship that some had rarely known, myself among them.

Because John was so alive, we could not believe there were cancer cells within his trim, athletic, thirty-eight-year-old body that would ultimately wreak havoc in his brain. The end came silently, after several long nights of brutal headaches and delirium. I joined his wife, his sons, and his mother in the ICU where machines were still pumping air into his lifeless body. His mother said she didn't think she could go in there, but when the time came, she could not stay away. She stood beside the body of her only son and watched her grandsons sob on their father's chest. It was the one and only time when John's lanky arms did not wrap themselves around his boys. As they kissed him good-bye I found myself clutching the cold, stainless steel railing of the bed in an attempt to draw strength from its unfeeling frame.

I prayed. The family left. The machines were turned off. I walked alone to the parking garage and climbed into my car. Turning the key in the ignition released my pent-up emotions. A stab of physical pain pierced through my chest so that I gasped for breath. I would say that I cried, but that's far too tame a word. I sobbed, I pounded my fist against the steering wheel, I shouted into the air-conditioned silence. There was no way around the pain. I was forced to speak, to cry, to shout what I felt, not what I thought I ought to say. The only word I remember shouting was, "No! No! No!" as the feelings flowed through me in all their delirious force.

I share that story not because it is unique, but because it is so common and because it is as close as I can get to the two great stories of sorrow of David's life. The first was the gruesome death of Saul and Jonathan, recorded in 1 Samuel 31. When David received the report of their demise, the man whose music had calmed Saul's troubled soul composed an eloquent psalm that he taught all the people to sing. It became their communal song of lament, like Elton John's singing "Goodbye, English Rose" at Princess Diana's funeral—only a whole lot better!

> Your glory, O Israel, lies slain upon your high places!
> How the mighty have fallen!
> . . . .
> You mountains of Gilboa,
> let there be no dew or rain upon you,
> nor bounteous fields!
> For there the shield of the mighty was defiled,
> the shield of Saul, anointed with oil no more.

. . . .

Saul and Jonathan, beloved and lovely!
  In life and in death they were not divided;
they were swifter than eagles,
  they were stronger than lions.

. . . .

Jonathan lies slain upon your high places.
  I am distressed for you, my brother Jonathan;
greatly beloved were you to me;
  your love to me was wonderful,
passing the love of women.

How the mighty have fallen,
  and the weapons of war perished!

(2 Samuel 1:19-27)

David's sad description of previously bounteous fields that no longer overflow with buds and flowers reminds me of the way Peter, Paul, and Mary taught my generation to sing "Where Have All the Flowers Gone?" If you're a child of the 1960s, you remember the way it goes from flowers to young girls, young girls to young men, young men to soldiers, soldiers to graveyards, graveyards to flowers. It's a melancholy sort of song. It sees life as a tragic cycle in which people make the same mistakes over and over again, always asking, "When will they ever learn?"

The second great sorrow in David's life was the death of Absalom, the fair-haired son David spoiled rotten but never understood. Absalom led a rebellion against his father. In the heat of the battle, Absalom's beautiful hair, symbol of his overreaching pride, became tangled in the branches of a tree. Dangling helplessly between heaven and earth, Absalom was run through by Joab's spears (2 Samuel 18:6-15). This time, David's grief took his breath away. He could not even sing. The loss was so dark and deep that David could do little more than utter his son's name.

The king was deeply moved, and went up to the chamber over the gate, and wept; and as he went, he said, "O my son Absalom, my son, my son Absalom! Would I had died instead of you, O Absalom, my son, my son!" (2 Samuel 18:33)

David wasn't the only father to say that. Let's look again at the story of my friend John. I was standing beside the elevator when his father, after whom he was named, arrived at the hospital. I knew "Brownie" as a cheerful, well-disciplined, retired military man, the kind who always stands up straight and offers a determined handshake as if to say, "I know who's in charge here." But when the elevator opened, he stepped through the door and collapsed in my arms as if the calcium in his bones had turned to powder and his muscles had been reduced to putty. He sobbed breathlessly as I held him in my arms. When he asked me why couldn't he have died instead of his son, I could hear the voice of David—crying over the death of his son Absalom.

The biblical writers never try to paper over the painful stuff of life. The truth about your life and mine is that every one of us will go through "the valley of the shadow" (Psalm 23:4 NIV). Sooner or later, every man is drawn into that deep, dark place of sorrow. It may be a death, a terrifying loss, or a monumental defeat. Whatever form it takes, sooner or later, every man must face the "dark night of the soul."

I learned a long time ago that the genuine tragedy in human life is not just that we suffer, but that there is sometimes suffering that never gets redeemed, suffering that does not result in deeper faith, a more sensitive heart, and a richer relationship with God. The question is not whether we will face sorrow. The question is, What can we learn from suffering? Will we have spiritual resources to enable us to move through it? By God's grace, how can our sorrow be redeemed?

One lesson we learn from David's sorrow is to honestly speak what we feel, to name our loss, to allow ourselves the time and space to experience our grief in all of its delirious force. Both of David's losses came when the kingdom was in the crisis of war, but in both events, everything stopped. There was a silent, empty space in which David and the people of Israel could embrace their loss and experience their sorrow.

> They mourned and wept, and fasted until evening for Saul and for his son Jonathan, and for the army of the LORD and for the house of Israel, because they had fallen by the sword. (2 Samuel 1:12)

> So the victory that day was turned into mourning for all the troops; for the troops heard that day, "The king is grieving for his son." (2 Samuel 19:2)

They gave themselves time to cry.

I must have been in fifth or sixth grade when my second cousin—a rambunctious farm kid who I remember as being willing to try almost anything—tried climbing to the top of an abandoned railroad water tank. He fell in and drowned. I remember the way the entire family gathered at their small frame home that summer afternoon. The women were crowded into the tiny, hot kitchen preparing food to spread on makeshift tables of sawhorses and planks. Men who always looked uncomfortable when they put on their suits and ties stood under the shade trees, talking about everything except the kid who had died. I remember the boy's father, awkwardly attempting to make conversation with the "city" cousins who had driven up from Pittsburgh for the funeral. But most of all, I remember what my dad said on the way home. With genuine sympathy for the boy's father, he said, "I wish he would go off in the woods and have a good cry."

This was one of the best lessons Dad taught me. David's sorrow teaches us to take time for a good cry.

David's way with sorrow also teaches us to search for God's presence in the midst of our sorrow, to look for some way that, through God's grace, the suffering can be redeemed. The biblical writer knows that God is at work behind, beneath, and through both tragedies to accomplish the relentless, redeeming purpose of God.

I don't believe that everything that happens to us is an expression of the purpose or will of God, but I do believe that God is able to be at work through everything that comes our way to accomplish his redeeming intention for us. Although every "thing" may not be the loving purpose of God, I am sure that there is no thing that can separate us from God's love. There is no thing that God cannot use as a part of his redemptive purpose in our lives and in our world. (See Romans 8:37-39.)

One night shortly after my friend John died, I had a dream. John was standing in my room. His presence was almost tangible. He seemed peaceful and calm. He said one thing to me: "It's okay, Jim. It's okay." It was so real that for an instant I thought his death had been the nightmare and that I was waking to discover that everything was back the way it should be. Then I came fully awake with a cold chill. My heart was beating, my eyes blurred with tears, and I was back in the real world where I had seen him die. A deep pain filled my chest as I silently cried, "It isn't okay. Things are not the way they should be."

A day later John's father met me at the front door of John's home, just around the corner from ours. He told me that he had had a dream in which John was telling him that he understood and that everything was okay. It did not take away his pain, but it gave him a moment of peace.

By faith, we could believe that things were "okay" with John, but things were clearly not okay for us. I do not believe that a death like his is the primary will of God. To the extent that death shatters the harmony and wholeness of human life, it is a frontal assault against the life-giving reign of God by the power of evil in our world, a world that has a lot more freedom in it than I would have permitted if I were God! The apostle Paul saw death as nothing less than "the last enemy" that resists the reign and rule of God (1 Corinthians 15:24-26). But by the power of God revealed in the resurrection of Jesus, even the pain of death can be used as a part of God's loving purpose in our lives.

But how does God do that? How does God go about the business of redeeming the sorrow, loss, and brokenness in our lives? The amazing word of the gospel is that God redeems our suffering, pain, and sin by taking it into himself in the death of Jesus on the cross. At the cross, the Almighty God knows how it feels for us to cry, "O Absalom, my son, my son."

The God in whom David trusted is not some kind of divine "Terminator," having all the power that anyone could want but lacking human passion, emotion, and tears. This is the God who *shares* human suffering, who knows the taste of human tears, who enters fully into our human weakness, all the way to the cross. The writer of the letter to the Hebrews described Jesus as "no High Priest who cannot sympathize with our weaknesses—he himself has shared fully in all our experience" (Hebrews 4:15 JBP). God redeems our sorrow, not from the outside in, but by sharing it from the inside out in the self-giving love of the cross.

Frederick Buechner, who says so many things so well, captured the power of the gospel in his reflections on the death of Absalom:

> When they broke the news to David, it broke his heart, just as simple as that, and he cried out in words that have echoed down the centuries ever since. "O my son Absalom, my son, my son. Would I had died instead of you."

He meant it, of course. If he could have done the boy's dying for him, he would have done it. If he could have paid the price for the boy's betrayal of him, he would have paid it. If he could have given his own life to make the boy alive again, he would have given it. But even a king can't do things like that. As later history was to prove, it takes a God.

(*Peculiar Treasures*, San Francisco: Harper & Row, 1979, p. 6)

The cross stands at the center of spirituality in the Christian tradition. There, the only Father who could give his son to die for us *did*. In the unfathomable, suffering love of God at the cross, our suffering is redeemed.

David's journey through sorrow also teaches us to move through sorrow into new life. Both of the great losses in his life created a crisis that God then used to shape the future (2 Samuel 2:1-4a; 19:11-15). The deaths of Saul and Jonathan opened the way for David to become king. The rebellion and death of Absalom prepared the way for Solomon to later become king and build the Temple. God brought new life out of the tragedy of death. When the darkness closes in around us, our challenge is to allow the experience of suffering to send us back into life as richer, warmer, stronger, more human, more loving men than we ever could have been before.

When my friend John went to the hospital, he received a get-well card from his best friend and coworker, the guy with whom he had traveled around the globe for Epcot Center, the soul-brother with whom he had spent many lonely nights and crowded days. On the outside of the card was a drawing of that irrepressible dreamer Don Quixote. Tall and skinny, he looked a lot like John. Beside him was his rotund, affable sidekick, Sancho, who bore a strange resemblance to the guy sending the card. On the blank inside page, John's friend had written, "Get well soon. We still have more windmills to tilt." It was signed, "Sancho."

There are always new windmills to tilt, new tasks to accomplish, new callings to pursue. There is always new life on the other side of the dark valley of sorrow, if only we have the spiritual vision to see it and the soul-strength to claim it.

More than a decade has passed since John's death. John's father died last year. There was a sense of peace in the assurance that the great wound that had been left in Brownie's heart by his only son's death had at last been healed. We claimed the promise that

God himself will be with them;
he will wipe every tear from their eyes.
Death will be no more;
mourning and crying and pain will be no more,
for the first things have passed away.
(Revelation 21:3b-4)

Some wounds can only be healed in the Resurrection. But along the way, other wounds have been healed and there have been wonderful gifts of new life. I've been at parties and family reunions that filled the house with laughter in which we could hear John's voice. I was there to perform the marriage of John's widow to a longtime friend. In their wedding service I read the words of David:

You have turned my mourning into dancing;
you have taken off my sackcloth
and clothed me with joy. (Psalm 30:11)

I was there to baptize their newborn son. I've seen John's boys move toward manhood, each in his own unique way exhibiting the energy and vitality their father gave them. And I've seen the gifts of John's friendship grow into deeper friendships with other guys whose lives were connected in their friendship with him.

My father's death came while we were preparing to break ground for the first phase of the building master plan for the newly organized congregation of St. Luke's United Methodist Church in Orlando. I took the architect's drawings with me on my last visit with him. He had made one visit to the vacant lot upon which the buildings would be constructed. We spread the drawings out on his hospital table. He studied them and said, "I'd sure like to live long enough to see this thing built." He paused for a moment, and then went on to say, "But I guess that's always how it is. I guess there's always something else you'd like to live a little longer to see." My father knew that there are always more windmills to tilt.

The tragedy in life is not that we experience sorrow. The tragedy is sorrow in which nothing is learned, suffering that never gets redeemed.

So, where is *your* place of sorrow? Where have you known those feelings that are so dark and deep that they must be shouted in all their honest, delirious force? What have you learned? And how will you allow the loving God to lead you from darkness into light?

> I cry aloud to God,
> aloud to God, that he may hear me.
> In the day of my trouble I seek the Lord;
> in the night my hand is stretched out without wearying;
> my soul refuses to be comforted.
> I think of God, and I moan;
> I meditate, and my spirit faints.
>
> (Psalm 77:1-3)

Time Out

S
O
R
R
O
W

1. *Weighing the time.* Shakespeare said, "The weight of this sad time we must obey; / Speak what we feel, not what we ought to say." Name the "sad time" in your life. When have you experienced pain, loss, or sorrow in any way comparable to David's sorrow? Spend some time reliving that experience.

2. *Redeeming the sorrow.* What did you learn from your experience of sorrow? How can you relate to the lessons described here? Did you learn to speak your feelings? If so, in what ways? Were you able to search for God's presence in the sorrow? What did you find? How did you move through sorrow to new life? What helped or hindered you in learning those lessons?

3. *Standing at the cross.* Spend some time in reflection on Hebrews 4:15 and Isaiah 53:1-12. What difference does it make for your experience with sorrow to know that Jesus has experienced it with you? How does the love of God at the cross bring healing to your pain?

4. *Claiming the future.* How does your growing relationship with God enable you to come through sorrow to hope? What new tasks or opportunities is God placing before you?

5. *Prayer.* Although John Donne (1572–1631) was one of the greatest communicators of his day, his poetry can be downright challenging for us today. These words on the ascension of Christ into heaven, however, are worth the effort it takes to read them. They

S
O
R
R
O
W

speak to the profound joy and new life that the Resurrection brings out of the darkness of death.

Salute the last and everlasting day,
Joy at the uprising of this Sun, and Son,
Ye whose just tears, or tribulation
Have purely washed, or burnt your drossy clay;
Behold the Highest, parting hence away,
Lightens the dark clouds, which he treads upon,
Nor doth he by ascending, show alone,
But first he, and he first enters the way.
O strong Ram, which hast battered heaven for me,
Mild Lamb, which with thy blood, hast marked the path;
Bright Torch, which shin'st, that I the way may see,
Oh, with thy own blood quench thy own just wrath,
And if thy holy Spirit, my Muse did raise,
Deign at my hands this crown of prayer and praise.

Chapter Seven

Reverence

Doesn't Anyone Fear God Anymore?

2 Samuel 6

> It was the experience of mystery—even if mixed with fear—
> that engendered religion.
>
> —*Albert Einstein*

Spirituality is "in" among men these days. I guess that's a good thing. At least talk about spiritual experience doesn't have to fight its way through barriers of macho, rationalistic resistance to get a hearing, the way it did during the modern era that theologian and Bible scholar Eugene Peterson called "The Great Spiritual Depression" (*Subversive Spirituality*, Grand Rapids: Eerdmans, 1997, p. 33). Everywhere you turn these days, folks are talking about spirituality. But when I listen to the spiritual chatter of our culture, I have to agree with Roman Catholic psychologist Eugene Kennedy, who said that a whole lot of what floats around under the label of "spirituality" is little more than "McSpirituality, junk food for the soul" (*Context*, July 15, 1996, p. 5).

My own spin on Kennedy's colorful phrase is that "McSpirituality" is quick. Who has time these days to dig around in old recipe books, shop for quality food, and spend hours in the kitchen preparing a full-course meal? Fast-food spirituality doesn't get in the way of all the stuff that fills our calendars.

McSpirituality is cheap; it can be purchased with pocket change. Unlike the preparation of a gourmet dinner, it never competes with our payments on the really important things, like the latest gadget from "The Sharper Image."

McSpirituality is predictable. It's the same in Memphis or Moscow; you always know what to expect. There are no questions, doubts, mysteries, or surprises.

But there are problems with McSpirituality. One is that there is not enough nourishment in it to make you strong, healthy, and whole. Another problem is that spiritual junk food is designed for our convenience. It's too much about *us,* and not enough about *God.*

The God we meet in the Bible is a health-giving, soul-strengthening, life-nourishing alternative to the spiritual junk food of our time. The God whose purpose was being worked out in David's life is anything but easy, cheap, or predictable. This God doesn't fit into the impression that men often have of religion being custom-designed for people who are weak, guilt-ridden, not very smart, or paying their fire insurance premiums to a vengeful deity. This is the all-powerful, all-knowing, all-holy, all-demanding God; the One who is wholly "other" but who intersects human history in sometimes shocking and often unexpected ways. David's experience demonstrates that life in relationship with God is never easy, cheap, or predictable, but it is filled with rugged energy, muscular wholeness, and unpredictable wonder and surprise.

The case in point is a disturbing story from the pinnacle of David's reign. After Saul's death, David was crowned king at Hebron. Seven and a half years later, he took control of a tiny hilltop stronghold named Jerusalem, and in a bold break from the past, David made Jerusalem the center of his kingdom (2 Samuel 5:1-12). The only thing left was for David to consolidate the people's loyalty around his rule. That's when David (or the most creative political consultant since the guy who dreamed up the "Willie Horton" ads) remembered the ark. That's right, folks! We're talking about the one and only, all-time-original ark of the covenant—the ark Moses carried through the wilderness and Harrison Ford's Indiana Jones recovered in the movie *Raiders of the Lost Ark.*

The ark was the most potent political symbol in Israel's history. For a relative comparison of the ark's importance, imagine the Declaration of Independence, the Statue of Liberty, and the battle-torn flag that inspired Francis Scott Key to write "The Star-Spangled Banner," all loaded up together in a tour bus and traveling around the country with the voice of Kate Smith singing "God Bless America" in the background and the aroma of Mom's apple pie wafting through the air. As a patriotic symbol for the Hebrew people, the ark was even better than that! It was sure to put a lump in the throat and a tear in the eye of every citizen of David's kingdom.

The ark was even more powerful as a spiritual symbol. Director Steven Spielberg caught the power of it in that spectacular scene in *Raiders* in which the Nazis opened the ark. Earth-shaking power, blinding light, and billowing flame flowed from it. The flesh melted right off the bones of anyone who dared look at it. For the Hebrew people the ark held tremendous, terrifying, awesome power. They believed that on the top of the ark, right between the two carved angels, was the spot where the Lord God Almighty touched the earth in cosmic power. The ark represented the pure, uncorrupted, and undiluted power of holiness that no sinful human being could endure. It was just what David needed to let everyone know that God was confirming his reign.

The ark had been gathering dust in Abinadab's house for twenty years (1 Samuel 7:1-2). In a move that was as politically strategic as it was spiritually spectacular, David led thirty thousand troops there, loaded the ark onto an ox cart, and headed back toward Jerusalem. The whole event was grander than a ticker-tape parade through Times Square (2 Samuel 6:1-5).

Things were working out just the way David's "media advisors" had planned until Uzzah, who was not of the priestly line and therefore not permitted to touch the ark, saw the oxen stumble. He reached out to steady the ark, touched it, and instantly died (2 Samuel 6:6-7). Zap! He might as well have been standing in a bathtub and stuck his finger in the electric socket. Suddenly, David's carefully laid plan was disrupted by the unexpected, uncontrollable power of God.

The possible medical explanation might be easy enough: it was a psychosomatic response; given all that the Hebrews believed about the ark, Uzzah was so horrified by what he had done that he collapsed with a heart attack. But the spiritual significance of the story goes much deeper. Uzzah's shocking death was a vivid reminder of the power and holiness of the God who was at work in David's life, but who was beyond David's manipulation or control. It's a reminder we could use today.

One of the dangers of McSpirituality is that we become just a little too chummy with God. The infinite One becomes a safe, convenient, domesticated deity. The Almighty God is transformed into a cosmic Santa Claus whose primary purpose is to satisfy our desires, an eternal buddy who hangs around the bar waiting to give us support, or the cheerleader for our sense of self-worth. The Creator of heaven and earth is reduced to a flag-waving parade marshal for nationalistic self-interest. In a culture of junk-food spirituality, we need to be reminded that when the Bible talks about God, it's talking about Jehovah, the Lord of Hosts, the King of Glory (Psalm 24). Uzzah's untimely death forces the question upon us: Doesn't anyone really fear God anymore?

Donald McCullough diagnosed the ailment of our times in a book with the disturbing title *The Trivialization of God: The Dangerous Illusion of a Manageable Deity* (Colorado Springs: Navpress, 1995).

> Reverence and awe have often been replaced by a yawn of familiarity. The consuming fire has been domesticated into a candle flame, adding a bit of religious atmosphere, perhaps, but no heat, no blinding light, no power for purification. (p. 13)

The Gallup folks confirmed McCullough's analysis in a survey in which Christians and non-Christians alike ranked "following God's will" well behind "finding happiness" or "achieving personal satisfaction" as the primary reason for their belief in God. The picture emerged of a benign deity who does little more than "bless" people— a spiritual butler who waits to meet our needs. Most folks want a deity who exists to serve our purposes rather than one who calls us out of ourselves to serve a divine purpose in the world.

Evidently, we're all a lot like David. We believe in the power of God, just as David believed in God's presence in the ark. But like David, we want to have it our way. We want to use God's power to accomplish *our* purposes, rather than to allow God to use us to accomplish the purpose of God. We need to be reminded that the God who meets us in the Bible is not a safe, domesticated deity whose power can be managed to serve our ends, manipulated to accomplish our desires, molded into our likeness, or marshaled to bless our favorite cause. The Almighty God is not primarily here to serve our needs, but to claim us as a part of the fulfillment of God's redeeming purpose in human experience.

Christ Church United Methodist in Fort Lauderdale, Florida, has become a model for ministry for the twenty-first century. Its spiritual leader, Dick Wills, bears witness to a defining moment in his life and in the life of that church when he stopped asking God to bless what he was doing and started praying for God to align his life with what God was blessing. How often do we ask God to "bless" the things we have already decided to do, rather than experience God's blessing in searching for God's will? There is a difference between using God for our purposes and allowing God to use us for God's purpose.

David's response to the shocking revelation of God's power in the ark may help us discover what it will mean for us to live in obedience to that loving, relentless will of God. David's initial response over what appears to him to be injustice toward Uzzah is one of *anger* (2 Samuel 6:8); let's call it "moral outrage." This is the voice within us that shouts, "This isn't right! It isn't fair!" I am convinced that precisely to the degree we are controlled by the love of Christ (2 Corinthians 5:11-15), we can trust that voice to be the Spirit of God. A vigorous relationship with the Almighty God will move us toward compassionate anger at the suffering of others.

We've got to be careful here. It's easy enough to be angry. But the spiritual challenge is to be angry over the right things. We have more than enough angry men in our culture today, some of them venting their vindictive rage under the banner of the Christian faith. The problem is that most of their anger is tuned to the frequency of their own self-interest. It is meanness born out of a selfish desire to protect their interests from any perceived invasion by the interests of others. This kind of self-protective indignation is the direct opposite of compassionate moral outrage that is motivated by the love of God in Christ at work within us.

I only know one method for determining appropriate, Christlike moral outrage: I measure the degree to which my anger is rooted in perceived injustice toward myself, in contrast to my sensitivity to injustice toward other people—particularly people who have less of everything the world values than I. The biblical yardstick for moral behavior always takes into account the effects our actions have on the marginalized, the powerless, and the poor. This is the kind of compassion that, by a literal definition of the Greek verb, "moved the guts" of Jesus when he saw the hurts and hungers of the people who crowded around him (Matthew 9:36; Mark 8:2).

How do we move from selfish meanness to compassionate anger?

The only place to begin is with a living, growing relationship with the Bible. I do not mean simplistic proof-texting—looking through the Bible to find anything that will affirm our preconceived notions or prove our point. I mean immersing ourselves in the words, meaning, and spirit of the Scriptures until the pure, passionate, steadfast love of God burns so deeply within us that our hearts are broken by those things that break the heart of God. Jeremiah the prophet said it was like a "fire in [his] bones" that he would have liked to put out but could not extinguish. When the love of God in Christ takes control of our lives, we begin to see every person as one for whom Christ died (2 Corinthians 5:13-14).

Professor Gilbert James opened the hearts of a whole generation of seminary students—myself among them—to this kind of loving moral outrage. He used to say we do not really hear the gospel until it makes us angry. Professor James took us from the idyllic world of our seminary campus into the inner city of Chicago. We lived in a "skid row" mission. We walked with people on the street. We listened to the witness of people who were confronting economic and racial injustice in the spirit of Christ. The experience ignited within us at least a flickering flame of the pure, white-hot compassion of God for the suffering of the world.

David's second response is *fear* (2 Samuel 6:9). Samuel tells us that what David had seen was so frightening he refused to take the ark to Jerusalem. Instead, he unloaded it in the house of Obed-edom, where it remained for three months (2 Samuel 6:10-11). That's just how frightening the power and presence of God can be! When the writer of Proverbs—perhaps David's son and royal successor, Solomon—said, "The fear of the LORD is the beginning of wisdom" (9:10), he was not talking about neurotic, debilitating, life-crushing paranoia, or shaking in our boots over ghosts, ghouls, and things that go "bump" in the night. The biblical word for *fear* comes from the Hebrew root for "reverence."

Fear that gives birth to wisdom is profound reverence for the power of God, breathless wonder at the mystery of God, and a soul-cleansing awareness of the goodness of God. Wisdom begins with reverence for the God whom Harry Emerson Fosdick often addressed as "so high above us that we cannot comprehend thee and yet so deep within us that we cannot escape thee" (*A Book of Public Prayers,* New York:

Harper and Bros., 1959, p. 20). The God David met at the ark is not safe, but the God whose holiness struck Uzzah to the ground is very good; good enough to give us just a touch of bone-shaking reverence that contains an element of fear.

David's fear may reflect the kind of awe-filled reverence that goes with the responsibility of leadership. Thomas Jefferson described this kind of reverence when he penned the words that are carved into the wall of his memorial in Washington, D.C.: "I tremble for my country when I reflect that God is just, that his justice cannot sleep forever." Abraham Lincoln felt it when he said that the great question was not whether God was on our side, but whether we were on the side of God. Pulitzer-prize-winning novelist Annie Dillard said that it is the kind of fear we should experience every Sunday when we come to worship:

> The churches are children playing on the floor with their chemistry sets, mixing up a batch of TNT to kill a Sunday morning. It is madness to wear ladies' straw hats . . . to church; we should all be wearing crash helmets. Ushers should issue life preservers and signal flares; they should lash us to our pews. For the sleeping god may wake some day and take offense, or the waking god may draw us out to where we can never return. (*Teaching a Stone to Talk*, New York: Harper & Row, p. 40)

I experienced that kind of fearful reverence early one morning as I was jogging across the bridge from Davis Islands to the mainland, where Tampa's historic Bayshore Boulevard bends along the Hillsborough Bay into downtown. A low-pressure system was lingering in the Gulf of Mexico. It left the city shrouded in a thick fog. I was running earlier than usual; the familiar morning runners, walkers, bikers, and skaters may have been frightened away by severe weather warnings I had not heard. I remember an odd awareness of being utterly alone in the predawn darkness. At the top of the bridge, I looked down into the foggy mist beneath me. A shudder of fear ran down my spine. I felt as if I were hanging on the edge of an abyss where the earth fell away into infinite nothingness.

Back at my desk, I reread the words of a review of a new book of poetry by Amy Clampitt entitled *A Silence Opens*. The reviewer said that the poetry went "to the extreme edge of the sayable" and that "this edge-of-language position is exactly where religious experience begins" (*New York Times Book Review*, May 15, 1994, p. 26). The story of Uzzah's unexpected death takes us to one of those "edge-of-language" places in scripture. Although we cannot fully explain the event itself, the story invites us to experience the fearful reverence that is the beginning of spiritual wisdom.

David's third and final response in the story of the ark is *worship and praise*. It took three months for David to get through his anger and fear, but then he marched back to the house of Obed-edom, loaded the ark up again, and paraded into Jerusalem in a celebration that makes our solemn presidential inaugurations look dull by comparison. It sounds more like an early Hebrew version of the New Orleans Mardi Gras (2 Samuel 6:12-19)! Old Testament scholar Walter Brueggemann called the scene "unfettered, unashamed extravagance" (*Interpretation: First & Second Samuel*, Louisville: John Knox Press, 1990, p. 250).

Nothing was more extravagant than the way David danced before the Lord. Liturgically, David's dancing embodied the joy and gratitude of the entire nation. Personally, the way David released himself with naked abandon before the altar symbolized his total availability to the purpose of God. This was worship in which the people offered themselves to the soul-energizing power, the life-giving presence, and the history-shaping purpose of God.

Don't get hung up on David's dancing, the way his jealous wife did (2 Samuel 6:20-23). I grew up in a conservative Christian tradition where folks were quite willing to believe the ominous warnings contained in a classic text of Christian morality entitled *From the Ballroom to Hell*. Since then, I've decided that when someone asks, "Can Christians dance?" the only appropriate answer is, "Some can, and some can't."

David's jealous wife misses the point. With or without physical dancing, it's not too much to expect that a growing relationship with God will lead us to moments of extravagant praise in which we are lifted out of ourselves and know that we are here for something larger than our own self-interest. Along the journey of our faith, there will be moments of divine encounter when we have no doubt that the Almighty God has intersected with our human experience and is at work to accomplish God's relentless purpose of redemption through us. In ways that are consistent with our own personalities, each of us will have profound moments of self-awareness in which we stand naked before the greatness and holiness of God, stripped of all our human pretense and illusions of power. It is not too much to expect that we will experience a soul-level awareness that our life is in harmony with the divine calling for which God created us, and that this will be enough to set our spirits dancing with joy.

How does it happen? For some of us, it happens in corporate worship, even as it did for David. I have a preacher friend who prays before every worship service, "Lord, do something today that isn't in the bulletin." Sometimes—though not often enough—the Order of Worship becomes a vehicle through which we experience the presence and power of the Almighty God. It happened that way for a man who stopped me at the door of the church after a service that included "The Renewal of Baptismal Vows." He said that as he made his way to the altar and dipped his fingers into the baptismal water, he felt the Spirit of God move within him in a way that he did not remember experiencing since his adolescence.

For some of us, it happens as we gather around the Table to receive the bread and cup in the sacrament of the Lord's Supper. Charles Wesley, who wrote more than six thousand hymns for "the people called Methodists," described the sacrament in profoundly experiential terms as a primary means by which God's grace becomes a reality within the human soul. Watch for the graphic way Wesley prays for our human senses to see, feel, taste, and experience the presence of Christ in the bread and cup.

> Jesu, at whose supreme command
>   We now approach to God,
> Before us in thy vesture stand,
>   Thy vesture dipped in blood.
> Obedient to thy gracious word,
>   We break the hallow'd bread,
> Commemorate thee, our dying Lord,
>   And trust on thee to feed.
>
> Now, Saviour, now thyself reveal,
>   And make thy nature known;
> Affix the sacramental seal,
>   And stamp us for thine own:

The tokens of thy dying love
　O let us all receive;
And feel the quickening Spirit move,
　And sensibly believe.

The cup of blessing, blest by thee,
　Let it thy blood impart;
The bread thy mystic body be,
　And cheer each languid heart.
The grace which sure salvation brings,
　Let us herewith receive;
Satiate the hungry with good things,
　The hidden manna give.

The living bread sent down from heaven,
　In us vouchsafe to be;
Thy flesh for all the world is given,
　And all may live by thee.
Now, Lord, on us thy flesh bestow,
　And let us drink thy blood,
Till all our souls are fill'd below
　With all the life of God.

For some of us it happens in the deep, quiet place where we open ourselves to the Spirit of God. In the silence of our own souls, we hear a "still small voice" within us (see 1 Kings 19:11-12 KJV). It happened that way for the men in a fall retreat group I led in Central Pennsylvania. Each of us spent an hour alone in silence, along the bank of a gentle, rolling river with the scent of autumn in the air. When we returned, each man shared the way God had spoken to him.

For some of us it comes through other people who walk the road with us. In the pure passion of love, in the honesty of friendship, in soul-searching dialogue with other Christians, through the proclaimed Word, we know the unmistakable presence of the risen Christ, just the way two disillusioned disciples experienced him as they walked along the road to Emmaus (Luke 24:13-35). It often happens that way for me as I receive the gift of encouragement, correction, or support from one of my brothers or sisters in Christ.

The critical factor is not *how* we experience the presence of God, but *that* we experience the One who comes to us, not to be used to

accomplish our purposes, but to enable us to be a part of the fulfillment of God's purpose of holy, relentless, life-giving love in this world.
I can promise you this: Experience the Almighty God, and you'll never
be satisfied with spiritual junk food again!

> The LORD is king! Let the earth rejoice;
>> let the many coastlands be glad!
> Clouds and thick darkness are all around him;
>> righteousness and justice are the foundation of his throne.
> Fire goes before him,
>> and consumes his adversaries on every side.
> His lightnings light up the world;
>> the earth sees and trembles.
> The mountains melt like wax before the LORD,
>> before the Lord of all the earth.
> The heavens proclaim his righteousness;
>> and all the peoples behold his glory.
> All worshipers of images are put to shame,
>> those who make their boast in worthless idols;
> all gods bow down before him.
> . . . .
> For you, O LORD, are most high over all the earth;
>> you are exalted far above all gods
> . . . .
> Light dawns for the righteous,
>> and joy for the upright in heart.
> Rejoice in the LORD, O you righteous,
>> and give thanks to his holy name!

(Psalm 97)

Time Out

**R
E
V
E
R
E
N
C
E**

1. *Check your spiritual diet.* To what degree are you getting along on spiritual "junk food"? What will it mean for you to move toward a healthier spiritual diet?

2. *In search of the Almighty God.* Take another look at the story of Uzzah (2 Samuel 6:6-7). The fact that you are reading this book confirms that your experience of God's presence has not been as overwhelming as was his! But in terms of your own life, how have you experienced "the all-powerful, all-knowing, all-holy, all-demanding God; the One who is wholly 'other' but who intersects human history in sometimes shocking and often unexpected ways"? (Your experience need not be as dramatic or as hard to explain as Uzzah's in order for it to be valid in your life.)

3. *Controlled by love.* What makes you angry? Is your anger a response to perceived injustice toward yourself or injustice toward others? Read 2 Corinthians 5:11-15. How fully is your life controlled by the love of Christ?

4. *Finding fearful reverence.* C. S. Lewis wrote that "holy places are dark places. It is life and strength, not knowledge and words, that we get in them. Holy wisdom is not clear and thin like water, but thick and dark like blood" (*Till We Have Faces: A Myth Retold,* p. 50). How have you experienced that dark, holy place? How have you known "the fear of the Lord" (see Proverbs 1:2-7)? What demands your deepest reverence? How long has it been since you

REVERENCE

experienced breathtaking awe before the greatness of God?

5. *Dancing in praise.* How have you experienced the presence of the Almighty God? In worship? In silence? Through other people? What pretenses would you need to lay aside in order to dance with naked spiritual abandon before the altar of God?

6. *Making yourself available to God.* How are you experiencing the difference between using God for your purpose and allowing God to use you for God's purpose? How much of your life is available to God?

7. *Prayer:*

Eternal God, so high above us that we cannot comprehend thee and yet so deep within us that we cannot escape thee, make thyself real to us today!

We are tired of our littleness and would escape from the narrow limitations of our ordinary lives. . . . Help us to go back to ordinary tasks to do simple things in a redeeming way, to perform common responsibilities with an uncommon spirit, and to face a disordered world with triumphant souls. . . . Save the community of thy people from cowardly surrender to the world, from rendering unto Caesar what belongs to thee, from forgetting the eternal Gospel amid the temporal pressures of our troubled days. . . . According to our needs may the riches of thy grace in Christ descend on every one of us. Amen.

Harry Emerson Fosdick,
A Book of Public Prayers (pp. 20-21)

L o v e

The Steadfast Center

2 Samuel 7

> I still believe that love is the most durable power in the
> world. . . . He who loves is a participant in the being of God.
>
> —*Martin Luther King, Jr., "The Most Durable Power"*

One of the things my wife and I love about
living in Florida is that we are always near the water. The Gulf is on
one side, the ocean is on the other, and there are peaceful lakes and
lazy rivers in between. Maybe that's why I like the old parable about a
spiritual Seeker who went to visit the Wise Sage beside the sea. The
Seeker asked, "How can I find God?" The Wise Sage said nothing, but
walked out into the water with the Seeker in tow. He put his hands on
the Seeker's head, pushed him under the water and held him thrash-
ing beneath the waves until he nearly drowned. When the Seeker
leaped out of the water gasping for breath, the Wise Sage said, "When
you want God as much as you want air, you'll find God."

Psalm 63 describes this same desire for God using a desert analogy,
tailor-made for wandering nomads who knew the desperate, parching
thirst of the desert.

> O God, you are my God, I seek you,
>   my soul thirsts for you;
> my flesh faints for you,
>   as in a dry and weary land where there is no water.
>
> (verse 1)

Take your pick: Wet or dry, sea or desert, the parable and the psalm
both describe a deep spiritual hunger that will be satisfied with noth-

ing less than the life-giving presence of God. This is the most profound longing of the human soul. Saint Augustine said that God put salt on our tongues that we might be thirsty for God. He knew from his own experience that our souls are restless, wandering searchers until they find their rest in God. We will never be satisfied with anything less than a living relationship with God, although God knows we try! Southern novelist Walker Percy described his hunger for God by saying that "life is a mystery, love is a delight. Therefore, I take it as axiomatic that one should settle for nothing less than the infinite mystery and the infinite delight, i.e., God. In fact I demand it. I refuse to settle for anything less" (*Context,* July 15, 1990, p. 3).

The throbbing center of spirituality in the Christian tradition is this innate hunger for the Almighty God who is revealed through the words of scripture and who came among us in Jesus Christ. *God* is at the center, which means *we* are not. The practice of spiritual discipline is the process by which we turn our attention away from ourselves and focus our attention on God.

The dialogue that David initiates with God in 2 Samuel 7:18-29 is the spiritual center of David's story. In this passage of scripture, we stand on the continental divide of David's life, the high point of both his reign and his relationship with God. King David had just settled into his new palace. His enemies had been defeated. He had everything in place and under control. Yet he had been so busy climbing to the throne that he had not taken time to look around at what he had accomplished. He reminds me of a guy who told me, "I was so busy getting to the top that when I got there I didn't know where I was."

Then David realizes that while he has been living in a great house of cedar, the ark of the covenant remains sitting under a tacky canvas tent, just as it has since the days when Moses carried it through the wilderness. David thinks it is time to build a decent house for the ark, a religious facility to match up to the standards David has set with his royal palace.

On the surface David's plan sounds as though it springs from a noble desire to honor God; but David may have had a political motive as well. It was common practice for rulers in the ancient world to build a temple as a permanent residence for their patron god. This solidified their power by the direct linkage of the political and religious lives of the nation. Nathan, the prophet, blessed the idea; it probably seemed like a good arrangement for the religious leaders to be in close relationship with the king.

Whatever mixed motives may have been at work in David's soul, God's word is unmistakably direct. God speaks twice in this passage. Both speeches are introduced by the daunting phrase, "Thus says the LORD" (2 Samuel 7:5, 8). The first word from God stings with divine sarcasm bordering on contempt. If you don't believe me, read the words aloud and see how they feel.

> Thus says the Lord: Are you the one to build me a house to live in? I have not lived in a house since the day I brought up the people of Israel from Egypt to this day, but I have been moving about in a tent and a tabernacle. . . . Did I ever speak a word with any of the tribal leaders of Israel, whom I commanded to shepherd my people Israel, saying, "Why have you not built me a house of cedar?" (2 Samuel 7:5-7)

Beneath the political realities of temple-building and the sarcasm of God's response, there was an important biblical principle at work here. The Almighty God cannot be confined, pinned down, or boxed in by human efforts. The God we meet in the Bible is constantly on the move. This is the God whose very nature is freedom (2 Corinthians 3:17) and who is always doing some new thing (Isaiah 43:18-19). Years later, when God finally gave a building permit for a temple and the project first proposed by David was completed by his son, King Solomon was wise enough to pray, "The highest heaven cannot contain you, much less this house that I have built!" (1 Kings 8:27*b*).

Biblically speaking, any god who can be fully contained and totally defined in human categories would not be fit to be called God. At the center of biblically formed spiritual experience is the humility that comes from our encounter with the infinite God who cannot be confined to our finite experience. The God we most deeply seek to know is the God we can never fully explain.

My problem with some of the preachers I hear on the airwaves these days is not that they are necessarily wrong, but that they are too sure of themselves. They seem to have resolved all the mystery of God. They talk as if they know exactly how God will work and what God will do. They leave very little space for the freedom of the biblical God who is totally beyond our human comprehension or control.

On the other hand, my problem with the "new age" spirituality that fills so many bookstore shelves is that the divinity of which they speak is so ambiguous as to be unknowable in any meaningful way. Almost anything that feels "spiritual" or "supernatural" can be identified as God. The great, good news of the Bible is that the uncontainable, uncontrollable, humanly incomprehensible God has intersected our finite experience. The essential character of God has been revealed to us through God's actions in history. The life-giving Word of God has become flesh among us in Jesus Christ (John 1:1-14). We may not be able to predict everything that God will do, but we can know who God is.

The second word from the Lord of Hosts to David (2 Samuel 7:8-17) declares the concrete action of God in human experience with a bold series of "I" statements.

> "I took you from the pasture . . ."
> "I have been with you wherever you went . . ."
> "I will make for you a great name . . ."
> "I will appoint a place for my people . . ."
> "I appointed judges over my people . . ."
> "I will give you rest from all your enemies . . ."
> "I will raise up your offspring after you . . . and I will establish the throne of his kingdom forever . . ."
> "I will be a father to him, and he shall be a son to me . . ."
> "When he commits iniquity, I will punish him . . ."

These affirmations build to a grand crescendo when the Lord declares, "I will not take my steadfast love from him, as I took it from Saul."

You don't have to be an authority on English grammar to get the point. God is always the subject of the active verb. We're talking about *God's* action here. God always gets the first move. Christians in the spiritual tradition of John Wesley have a theological label for the loving initiative of God in human experience. We call it *prevenient grace,* meaning, the "grace that goes before." God's action is always prior to our response; God's grace creates the possibility of our obedience.

A few years ago a Christian organization handed out bumper stickers that proclaimed, "I FOUND IT!" While I celebrated the witness of people who had "found" new life in Christ, my problem was that the human "I" was the subject of the active verb. It gave the impression that God is lost, and that the human being is the spiritual search party who goes out to find God, when the Bible tells the story exactly the other way around.

This business of searching for God took a humorous twist last year when the Assembly of God in Bushnell, Florida, received one of those computerized letters from the American Family Publishers. It announced that "God, of Bushnell, Florida," had been chosen as a finalist for the $11 million top prize in the American Family Publishers Sweepstakes. The letter declared:

> GOD, we've been searching for you! What an incredible fortune this would be for you, GOD! Could you imagine the looks you'd get from your neighbors! But don't just sit there, GOD!

The letter went on to tell God how to send in the appropriate form to receive the prize.

The computer's attempt to contact "GOD" is no less humorous than our thinking that *we* are the ones who find *God*. The Bible says that the initiative moves in exactly the opposite direction. From the moment God came searching for Adam and Eve as they hid in the garden (Genesis 3:8-10) to the story Jesus told of the shepherd who went searching for the lost sheep (Luke 15:4-7), the Bible is very clear that we are the ones who are lost, and God searches for us. Indeed, the final prayer in the Bible is the first prayer of our spiritual journey: "Come, Lord Jesus!" (Revelation 22:20). All of our seeking and any of our finding is our response to the God who seeks us, finds us, and claims us by the initiative of divine love. The homesickness of our souls is the sign of God's prevenient grace at work in our experience.

An anonymous hymn-writer described the surprising realization of who does the seeking and finding in these words:

> I sought the Lord,
> and afterward I knew
> he moved my soul to seek him, seeking me.
> It was not I that found, O Savior true;
> no, I was found of thee.

I pulled up my e-mail one day and was surprised to see a message from a man who had been a kid in my youth group many years ago.

Listen for the prevenient grace of God that began in his life back then and is coming into fulfillment today.

> I was surfing websites this morning and had to say hello. It is really strange that I found your address, because I was thinking about you just last week. God has really touched my life in a personal and fulfilling way. So much so that I have begun to answer His call to go into full-time ministry. He has given me so much and forgiven so much that I don't even know where to begin. I teach a Sunday school class, volunteer with the youth, and lead a men's Bible study and prayer group. I was telling the confirmation class (we have 35 kids!!) about the class that I was in on your back porch. I thought we had maybe five but I wasn't sure. Boy, that is a great memory. I just wanted to say thanks for your witness and guidance. Goes to show that planted seeds do blossom if they are planted with care and God's love.

The culminating "I" statement from the Lord made an astounding promise: "I will not take my *steadfast love* from him" (2 Samuel 7:15, italics added). This same phrase shows up in Psalm 63, where David describes his experience of the God for whom his soul is thirsting:

> I have looked upon you in the sanctuary,
>   beholding your power and glory.
> Because your *steadfast love* is better than life,
>   my lips will praise you.
>   (Psalm 63:2-3, italics added)

The Hebrew word for the phrase "steadfast love" is *hesed*. It carries a sense of passionate, persistent loyalty. It is an expression of the relentless, loving will of God. In *God Isn't Finished with Us Yet* (Nashville: The Upper Room, 1991), I defined *hesed* as "The Love That Just Won't Quit." The classic picture of *hesed* in the Old Testament is the prophet Hosea, whose wife, Gomer, left him and entered into a life of prostitution. But Hosea never stopped loving her. He pursued her, followed her, spent his wealth to buy her off the auction block. Hosea's persistent love became the prophetic portrayal of *hesed*, the steadfast love of God for spiritually unfaithful people who run from God. The prophet hears the voice of God, like loving parents crying over their run-away children:

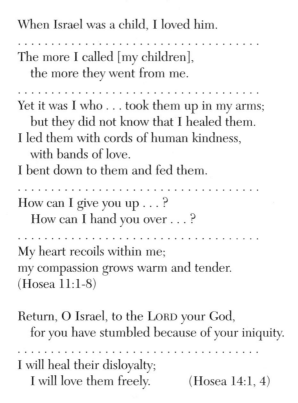

When Israel was a child, I loved him.
. . . .
The more I called [my children],
    the more they went from me.
. . . .
Yet it was I who . . . took them up in my arms;
    but they did not know that I healed them.
I led them with cords of human kindness,
    with bands of love.
I bent down to them and fed them.
. . . .
How can I give you up . . . ?
    How can I hand you over . . . ?
. . . .
My heart recoils within me;
my compassion grows warm and tender.
(Hosea 11:1-8)

Return, O Israel, to the LORD your God,
    for you have stumbled because of your iniquity.
. . . .
I will heal their disloyalty;
    I will love them freely.   (Hosea 14:1, 4)

That's *hesed.* That's what the Bible means by the steadfast love of the Lord. And that's the kind of steadfast love God declared would be at the everlasting core of God's relationship with the house of David. It's not as if David and his heirs would no longer be accountable for their behavior. God promised to punish them "with blows inflicted by human beings" when they were disobedient to the loving purpose of God (2 Samuel 7:14). God will use the logical consequences of human behavior as the instrument of spiritual discipline. As we will see in the rest of David's story, the promise of God's steadfast love does not cancel out the human consequences of stupid, selfish, and sinful choices. But the divine *hesed*—the steadfast and everlasting love of God—will be the nonnegotiable, persistent reality at the core of God's relationship with humankind.

Let's face it: most men have a difficult time using the word *love*. I suspect this is because the term has been softened by mushy "love" songs, cheapened to soap opera status by "love" stories, and weakened by shallow "chick flick" movies. Many men have nearly decided the only reason they should be interested in that stuff is that it might be a good way to get a woman into bed! The word *love* has been so loaded down with rosebuds and lace that it's difficult for a man to use the word to define an identifiable reality in his own life, with the possible exception of the love of mother, country, and a favorite dog.

But there is nothing wimpy or effeminate about *hesed*. The steadfast love of the Lord is a robust, muscular, unwavering loyalty that wills to continue loving regardless of the cost. It is not based on feelings but is expressed in action. (See 1 Corinthians 13 and 1 John.) It is nothing short of the love of God revealed in the life of Jesus and demonstrated in the way he went to the cross. Jesus made it perfectly clear that the nonnegotiable core of the Christian life is loving God with all our heart, soul, mind, and strength (Matthew 22:37; Mark 12:30; Luke 10:27), which doesn't sound like wimpy stuff to me! The "new commandment" to Jesus' followers was to love people the way Christ loved us (John 13:34), which is no walk in the park either! John Ortberg spoke of this love in words that have become a basic part of my approach to ministry:

> Jesus consistently focused on people's *center:* Are they oriented and moving *toward* the center of spiritual life (love of God and people), or are they moving *away from* it? (*The Life You've Always Wanted*, Grand Rapids: Zondervan, 1997, p. 37, italics his)

In my personal spiritual discipline and in my pastoral leadership, I have been attempting to move to the center; to intentionally focus my life on the central core of loving God and loving others in the Spirit of Christ from the inside out. It hasn't been easy. I am easily distracted by all sorts of secondary, outside-in issues. But I am finding new freedom, power, and joy in disciplining myself to intentionally focus on the center; to ground my life more and more firmly in the love of God revealed in Christ.

God's address to David provides the context for David's response, which begins with a soul-level cry of honest humility: "Who am I, O Lord God, and what is my house, that you have brought me thus far?" (2 Samuel 7:18).

Our response to God's initiative always involves the realization of who we are as finite, human creatures in the presence of the infinite

God. It calls us to lay aside all of our attempts to hide, protect, or deny our human weakness. It means discovering the freedom that comes in being honest about who we really are.

Across the twelve years President Franklin Delano Roosevelt was in the White House, the entire nation participated in what one writer called "a splendid deception" with regard to his polio. The American people had no idea that their president could not stand without the braces on his legs. The nation never saw his wheelchair. Not a single photograph revealed any of the president's weakness.

The charade came to an end on March 1, 1945. A joint session of Congress had packed the House chamber to hear the president report on the Yalta Conference. The doorkeeper announced, "The President of the United States." An awe-stricken hush settled over the chamber when the door opened and they saw the president seated in his wheelchair. For the first time, he allowed himself to be wheeled down the aisle. Instead of being propped up behind the lectern, he seated himself in a chair below the dais. The crowd listened in wonder as he said, "I hope you will pardon me for the unusual posture of sitting down during the presentation of what I want to say, but I know that you will realize that it makes it a lot easier for me in not having to carry about ten pounds of steel around on the bottom of my legs." Roosevelt's long-time assistant, Frances Perkins, remembered, "It was the first reference he had ever made to his incapacity. . . . I remember choking up to realize that he was actually saying, 'You see, I'm a crippled man.' He had never said it before. . . . He had to bring himself to full humility to say it before Congress." Doris Kearns Goodwin described the impact of the moment:

> The energy required to sustain the deception was no longer there. . . . Freed from the burden of his braces, Roosevelt delivered an intimate, chatty address. . . . And now, for a brief moment, the entire chamber was allowed to see what Roosevelt's colleagues had always seen. But rather than lessening their regard for him, as Roosevelt had always feared it might, this glimpse of Roosevelt's vulnerability only magnified the power and charm of his personality. (*No Ordinary Time*, New York: Simon and Schuster, 1994, pp. 586-87)

A genuine experience of God's presence in our lives invites us to experience the liberating humility in which we lay aside the pretense and posturing of our pride and simply acknowledge who we are before God and others.

Most of us understand the country song that complains, "Lord, it's hard to be humble when you're perfect in every way." We are a lot like the guy who said, "I've mastered the virtue of humility and I'm damn proud of it." It's hard to be humble, but it's even harder to maintain the deception of self-sufficiency. It takes tremendous energy to hold up the façades we erect to protect ourselves from the truth of our humanity. The evidence of scripture and the witness of human experience is that if we are to receive the gifts that God has to give, we must learn the lesson of humility.

My clergy cronies and I experience that gift in our annual retreats. Every year, one or more of us comes to our time together with a deep need to let down our defenses, to clear away the façades of success, and to be ruthlessly honest about the real needs of our lives. And in an amazing way, each of us has discovered the freedom that comes from genuine humility and the healing that comes through acceptance and grace. Rather than weakening us, our vulnerability has become a source of strength.

Out of his humility, David's response to God moves to joy-soaked thanksgiving. He recites the ways in which God has blessed his house, building to his shout of praise, "Thus your name will be magnified forever in the saying, 'The LORD of hosts is God over Israel' " (2 Samuel 7:26). We might label this "the attitude of gratitude" (this may sound trite, but at least it's memorable). Every person I know who is spiritually alive demonstrates a profound sense of gratitude for every gift that comes into his or her life from God. Karl Barth, whose faith was forged on the anvil of resistance to Nazi power, used two Greek terms to describe the connection between grace (*charis*) and thanksgiving (*eucharist*).

> *Charis* always demands the answer *eucharistia* (that is, grace always demands the answer of gratitude). Grace and gratitude belong together like heaven and earth. Grace evokes gratitude like the voice an echo. Gratitude follows grace as thunder follows lightening. (*A Long Obedience in the Same Direction*, Downers Grove, Ill.: InterVarsity Press, 1980, p. 192)

I've only had one wife, but I'm on my third wedding ring. The first had to be cut off after a water skiing accident in which I could have lost the finger as well. The second disappeared when I dove into the azure blue but surprisingly cold water off the coast of Brazil. Shrinkage, I guess! I'm trying to take better care of the third one. The first ring, the one Marsha gave me at our wedding, was engraved with a paraphrase of James 1:17, "Every good and perfect gift comes from God." I've never had the nerve to ask if that meant that I was God's good and perfect gift to her or if she were God's good and perfect gift to me! I think it meant that the gift of this relationship, this human love, was not something we had earned or deserved. It is something we have worked very hard to maintain, but the relationship itself is a gift, freely given to us by God. Our task has been to receive, nurture, and strengthen it, out of profound gratitude for the loving gift of God in our lives.

To live out of the spiritual center of our lives is to develop a constant awareness that the good things in our lives have not been earned, made, shaped, or determined by our human powers but have been freely given to us by a generous, loving God.

In the final movement of his response, David's prayer turns to audacious boldness. He calls upon God to complete the promise God has made for his life, to fulfill God's good purpose in and through his life (2 Samuel 7:25). I've become pretty well convinced that there are only two things that can block the flow of God's steadfast love in our lives. One is the illusion of self-sufficiency. Any time we start to think that we are autonomous masters of our fate who can make it on our own, we're headed for trouble. (We'll see this soon enough in David's story.) The other thing that can get in the way of God's Spirit at work within us is the pain of inadequacy: the inner fear and insecurity that robs us of the "holy boldness" with which David dares to lay claim to God's promise in his life. This kind of insecurity is usually a result of a twisted sort of self-protective pride, a deep fear of being known for who we really are. Sometimes it is the long-term conditioning in dysfunctional families that makes it almost impossible for us to believe that we could be loved. Whatever the cause, the result is that we lack the courage of faith that humbly and gratefully claims the promise of God for our lives.

Our daughters were less than six months old when we took each of them to the altar of the church and offered them to God in the sacrament of baptism. We took vows expressing our promise as their parents and as the church to be faithful to God and to raise them in "the way that leads to life." The water that was placed on their heads was the sign of God's promise to be faithful to them. With all of our human weaknesses and failures, we've done our best to be faithful to the promises we made. But as the girls have grown into women, we've realized that the promises God made to us are infinitely more important than the promises we made to God. There have been many times when we have prayed, "Lord, we gave them to you at their baptisms, and we aren't taking them back now. They belong to you, and we are depending on you to fulfill your promise in their lives." Across the years, we have seen amazing ways in which God has been faithful to the promise of love and grace. We have discovered the boldness with which David prayed that God would do what God had promised in them.

This soul-level dialogue, which stands at the very center of David's story, focuses our spiritual journey in the central reality of God's steadfast love. To find God means being found by Divine Love, so that the love of God becomes the life-giving force at the central core of our existence. Only the steadfast love of God, which was supremely revealed at the cross, will satisfy the deepest hunger and thirst of our souls.

> My soul is satisfied as with a rich feast,
>   and my mouth praises you with joyful lips
> when I think of you on my bed,
>   and meditate on you in the watches of the night;
> for you have been my help,
>   and in the shadow of your wings I sing for joy.
> My soul clings to you;
>   your right hand upholds me.
>
> (Psalm 63:5-8)

Time Out

S
T
E
A
D
F
A
S
T

L
O
V
E

1. *How thirsty are you?* How have you experienced a soul-thirst or spiritual hunger for God? How have you attempted to answer that thirst with other things?

2. *How big is your God?* Where do you fall on a continuum between folks who seem to have all the answers and those for whom God is "so ambiguous as to be unknowable in any meaningful way"?

3. *How has God searched for you?* How has God's "prevenient" grace—the "grace that goes before"—been operative in your story?

4. *How steadfast is your love?* Do you have difficulty talking about love? Does talk of love seem wimpy or effeminate to you? Why do you think this is the case for some men? How have you observed God's love as a "robust, muscular, unwavering loyalty that wills to continue loving regardless of the cost?"

5. *How's your humility?* Here's the way one of the readers of the manuscript of this book responded to the story of Franklin Roosevelt:

   I have spent years with "spiritual braces" on my legs, so that when others see me they might think I am right with the Lord. If after all these years I remove them, not only am I afraid I will be "found out," but without some kind of conditioning and training, I will simply fall on my face. How do I make that leap? I know intellectually that it's a "step," but it sure feels like a "leap." (Personal correspondence)

**S
T
E
A
D
F
A
S
T

L
O
V
E**

Can you identify with this man's feelings? How would you answer his question: "How do I make that [spiritual] leap?" (My response would include not attempting to do it alone: "When you're ready to take off the braces, do it with a soul-friend who can help you learn to walk in a new way.")

6. *How's your "attitude of gratitude"?* When was the last time you were knocked off your feet by some deep, inner awareness of God's generosity toward you? Describe that experience. What are you doing to nurture that "attitude of gratitude" in your life?

7. *How bold are you?* What will it mean for you to claim the promise that God will fulfill God's good purpose in your life?

8. *How stable is your center?* What is the centripetal center around which everything else in your life revolves? How is your life being shaped by the steadfast love of God?

9. *Prayer:*

> Jesus, thine all-victorious love
>   Shed in my heart abroad;
> Then shall my feet no longer rove,
>   Rooted and fixed in God.
>
> O that in me the sacred fire
>   Might now begin to glow;
> Burn up the dross of base desire
>   And make the mountains flow!
>
> O that it now from heaven might fall
>   And all my sins consume!
> Come, Holy Ghost, for thee I call,
>   Spirit of burning, come!

S
T
E
A
D
F
A
S
T

L
O
V
E

Refining fire, go through my heart,
Illuminate my soul;
Scatter thy life through every part
And sanctify the whole.

Charles Wesley

Chapter Nine

Sin

Fatal Attraction

2 Samuel 11

> We win our souls after long years of practicing the disci-
> pline of awareness and abiding in fear and trembling until we
> learn, at last, to rest content with our grandeur and baseness.
>
> —*Sam Keen,* Fire in the Belly

There was a time when I got a kick out of telling the story of David's lusty affair with Bathsheba and his clever manipulation of Uriah. The tantalizing tale pulsates with sex and passion, deceit and murder. There's even a touch of satire and irony in it. But I was reluctant to turn the corner this time. I knew what was out ahead, and I wasn't at all sure I wanted to go through it again.

Perhaps I hesitated because I'm older now. I've been through my own midlife crisis (thankfully, without Bathsheba!) and written a book about it. Perhaps I hesitated because I've been down this road often enough to know how susceptible we all are to the temptations of power, and I know the pain it causes. Perhaps, with the writer of the biblical text, I have begun to see the story more in terms of its long-term consequences than its immediate intrigue. Or perhaps I hesitated because there was something in me that wanted to freeze the action, to look for some way to change what happened to David, or, at least, to prevent it from happening to someone else.

This is a man's story, told from a man's perspective. By the time it took written form, the Spirit of God had honed and polished it in the process of being told and retold from generation to generation. The Hebrew people treasured this story because it helped them under-stand what happened to David, and it helped them understand themselves. Old Testament scholar Walter Brueggemann said of the story that it forces us to confront the hard "questions of human desire and human power—desire with all its delight, power with all its potential for death. . . . This narrative is more than we want to know about David and more than we can bear to understand about ourselves" (*Interpretation: First and Second Samuel*, Louisville: John Knox Press, 1990, p. 272). He described it as the painful reality of living with "too much power coupled with too little self-doubt" (p. 266). It has the potential of unmasking the temptations that lurk within each of us.

Srully Blotnick studied six thousand men over a period of twenty-five years to answer the question "What is success for the American male?" Blotnick published his results in a book entitled *Ambitious Men: Their Drives, Dreams, and Delusions* (New York: Viking, 1987). He concluded that we define success in terms of fortune, fame, power, and prestige. For American males, success is measured quantitatively, primarily by dollars and cents. Blotnick confirmed that the ambition that drives us is the desire for more. If we ask, "More what?" the answer is simply more of what we already have. More money, more fame, more power, more prestige.

By Blotnick's description, David had it made! He was a middle-aged man at the top of his game. He had risen from obscurity to the pinnacle of power. He had consolidated a bunch of fragmented tribes into one united nation with "justice and equity [for] all" (2 Samuel 8:15). David's armies were victorious over their enemies. Even by the biblical definition of success that we considered earlier in his story, David had clearly arrived. He was the king, just as God had intended. It doesn't get any better than this. All he wanted was more!

Sherman McCoy is a contemporary copy of David. He is the central character in Thomas Wolfe's best-selling novel *The Bonfire of the Vanities*. Sherman McCoy had made it to the top on Wall Street. As he strode through Manhattan, he felt like a "master of the universe." He lived in a $2 million Park Avenue apartment. He drove an expensive foreign car, belonged to the right clubs, and had an attractive wife at home and a daughter in the best private school. All he wanted was more. But Sherman McCoy also had a mistress. One night, with her in his car, he made one wrong turn and ended up in the Bronx. That mistake set in motion a flood of consequences he never expected and could not control. This is what happened to David.

It was springtime, the writer tells us, the time when most kings went to battle. But David no longer marched with his troops. There was a time when he was forced to depend upon the power of God because the challenges he confronted were so much larger than his own ability or strength. But those days were behind him. The story opens at a leisurely pace. David is at ease in what the demonic Tempter in *The Screwtape Letters* described as "the long, dull, monotonous years of middle-aged prosperity," which Screwtape claimed as "excellent campaigning weather" (C. S. Lewis, *The Screwtape Letters*, p. 143).

There's an important reminder for us here. The times when we are up against the wall of our own inadequacies are generally not the times we turn away from God. They are opportunities for us to grow into a deeper, stronger, more vigorous awareness of God's presence. When life is easy, when everything seems to be going our way, when there are no difficult struggles to face, we are easily tempted to take our faith for granted and to allow our souls to grow flabby by the neglect of spiritual discipline. It was springtime for David, and the livin' was easy.

> Late one afternoon, when David rose from his couch and was walking about on the roof of the king's house . . . he saw from the roof a woman bathing; the woman was very beautiful. (2 Samuel 11:2)

Nothing unusual there. David was not the first or last man to notice a beautiful woman. I've never quite understood all the hoopla about former President Jimmy Carter's once saying he had committed adultery in his heart. So, who hasn't? Show me a healthy, heterosexual, red-blooded male who says he's never noticed a beautiful woman, and I'll show you a liar! The old country proverb says that it's one thing for the birds of temptation to fly over your head, but it's another thing to let them build a nest in your hair. "Adultery in the heart" wasn't enough for David. After all, he was the king! He was a "master of the universe." He could have whatever he wanted, and he wanted more. "David sent someone to inquire about the woman. It was reported, 'This is Bathsheba daughter of Eliam, the wife of Uriah the Hittite' " (v. 3). If only that had been the end of the story!

It's been over a decade since the release of the movie *Fatal Attraction,* but some of my preacher friends still say that this film was more effective than any of their sermons in causing men to think twice about committing adultery. *Time* magazine called it "a homily for our times" (November 16, 1987; p. 79). *Fatal Attraction* was David's story projected against the sexual mores of our culture. In the movie, Dan (Michael Douglas) is a successful businessman whose wife (Anne Archer) and daughter are away for the weekend. Dan meets the lusciously lascivious Alex (Glenn Close) at an office party, and they sneak off for a private drink. Toying with his obvious lust, she calls him a "naughty boy." He protests that he is a happily married man, to which she responds, "So, what are you doing here?"

Things would have been a lot happier for Dan, his wife, his daughter, and her pet rabbit if the story had ended right there. Dan's decision at that moment would wreak havoc in all of their lives. That's just how life is. Major consequences often flow from what seem to be small decisions. The path toward immoral behavior usually begins with small steps. The early choices make the difference.

That's where it should have ended for David and Bathsheba, as well. But there were no boundaries for the king when he wanted more and had the power to get it. The pace of the story quickens. The active verbs rush toward the climax of David's lust. "David sent messengers to get her, and she came to him, and he lay with her. . . . Then she returned to her house" (v. 4).

David thought it was over; just an afternoon of sexual pleasure. After all, that's what real men with real power do. When they want something, they take it with no restraints, no delay, no second thoughts, no consideration of anything beyond their own lust for more. But life is never that simple. With graceful restraint but blinding force, the text records, "The woman conceived; and she sent and told David, 'I am pregnant' " (v. 5). Suddenly, David has a problem, but there's no sign that David was overly concerned. After all, he was in control; he could work this out. David sent for Bathsheba's husband, Uriah, listened to his report on the battle, and then told him, "Go down to your house, and wash your feet" (vs. 6-8).

I'm sure David spoke those words with a wink of his eye and a manly elbow in Uriah's ribs. "Wash your feet" was a Hebrew euphemism for sexual intercourse. That's clearly what David intended. But David had not counted on Uriah's integrity. Uriah felt it would be a dishonor to his fellow soldiers to go home to the pleasures of his wife while they risked their lives and endured the hardships of the battlefront. Instead of going home, Uriah camped out in the king's barracks with the rest of the king's men. The next morning, David tried again to get Uriah to go home to his wife, but again Uriah refused. This didn't stop the king. The next day, he invited Uriah to dinner and got him drunk; but even with a hangover, Uriah did not "go down" to his house (v. 13).

Don't miss that little phrase, "go down," which has come to have its own lascivious meaning in our contemporary culture. The writer of 2 Samuel uses it five times in eight verses. To David's great frustration, he could not make Uriah "go down." Have you ever noticed that when you "go down" on your integrity, you expect everyone else to "go down" on theirs? If you start to lie, you expect everyone else to lie. If you cheat, you expect everyone else to cheat. If you're greedy, mean, and selfish, you expect everyone else to be exactly the same. And have you noticed how frustrating it is to run into someone who simply refuses to "go down" with you?

If David could not get what he wanted by seduction, he could still get it with raw, royal power. He sent Uriah back to the front with a direct order for his field commander to "set Uriah in the forefront of the hardest fighting, and then draw back from him, so that he may be struck down and die" (v. 15). David wrote the order in his own hand. In the Watergate era, we called that a "smoking gun." Field Commander Joab followed the king's command, and Uriah was killed in battle. As soon as an appropriate time of mourning passed, "David sent and brought [Bathsheba] to his house, and she became his wife, and bore him a son" (v. 27). The curtain drops on this episode of the soap opera with everything apparently in place and conveniently under David's control.

You may be thinking, This is a tantalizing tale, but what does it have to do with men's spirituality? What does this story of sex and power teach me about living from the inside out in my relationship with God? The odds are good that most of the men who read this book will not stoop to the level of betrayal portrayed in David's seductive affair with Bathsheba and his odious murder of Uriah. If that were all this story were about, most of us could walk away from it unscathed, untouched, and unchanged. Where can we find ourselves in this story?

The Hebrew storytellers were not only inspired, they were also masters of their trade. If you read the text carefully you will discover that the word *God* never appears in 2 Samuel 11. David is almost always the subject of the active verb. The God who until now has been so actively involved in David's life is never even mentioned. It's a long and winding road from the story of David and Goliath that was told "so that all the earth may know that there is a God in Israel" (1 Samuel 17:46), through the declaration of God's action in the "I" statements in 2 Samuel 7:8-17, to this tale of abused royal power in which God's presence is never acknowledged and David's self-centered lust determines all his actions.

The story is too perfectly told for the absence of any reference to God to be anything other than a dramatic reminder of the lengths to which a man can go when he is infected with "too much power and too little self-doubt" (Brueggemann, p. 266). The story becomes our story when we realize that it is ultimately about the apparent absence of God as a living, active, controlling presence in human life. David's actions uncover the depths to which a man can fall when he becomes so confident in his own powers that he no longer lives out of a soul-centering experience of the presence of the living God. This is the dramatic description of what happens when we attempt to live by what one business consultant called the "EGO Factor," for "Edging God Out." This is what life comes to when we attempt to live autonomously, with no vital awareness of our dependence upon God or our accountability to others.

While Hitler was gobbling up Europe in the late 1930s, British poet W. H. Auden surprised the literary world by returning from agnosticism to Christian faith. He said one of the things that led him in that direction was the realization that the only philosophical argument that could counter the Nazi ideology was rooted in religious faith. Auden discovered that, as Dostoyevsky said, "If there is no God, all things are permissible" (*New York Times Book Review*, March 31, 1996; p. 9). If there is no God to whom we are accountable and if the only criterion for our actions is whether they accomplish what we desire, there are ultimately no boundaries for our behavior. Anything goes.

The only reliable measuring stick for my life from the outside in is the depth to which I live from the inside out. The degree to which I can be trusted is precisely the degree to which I have cultivated an awareness of the presence of God in my life. Or to say it negatively, the degree to which I attempt to live autonomously, guided by nothing other than my own desires, is also the degree to which I am controlled by the self-centered ambition that the Bible defines as the root of sin (Genesis 3:5). And that's where this story begins to tell us more about ourselves than we may want to know.

As a young pastor, I was shocked and offended by a fellow pastor who "went down" on his sexual integrity. My reaction was one of moral indignation, which I unloaded with idealistic fervor on an older, wiser, more experienced pastor friend. He listened to my tirade with amazing patience. When I finished, he was silent for a moment. I still remember the way he scratched his balding head and worked his jaw like a cow chewing her cud. He looked me straight in the eye, and with genuine compassion in his voice, he replied, "You know, Jim, I've come to the point that when I see this kind of thing happen to someone else, it reminds me of what I might be capable of doing too." My friend taught me to see the very real possibilities for disaster in my own life if I did not maintain a growing, intimate relationship with God and faithful accountability to others. This is a lesson I've remembered for twenty-five years. It's a part of the lesson we can carry from the tragic story of self-satisfying lust in the life of President Clinton in his affair with Monica Lewinsky.

If I have not given attention to God's presence at the center of my personality; if I am not cultivating the love of God in Christ as the controlling reality in my daily experience; if the desire to be obedient to God's will is not the overriding desire that determines my actions; if I am not living with a practical sense of accountability to God and to others, I will inevitably begin to act as if I am the autonomous master of the universe. My perceived needs and passions will take precedence over everything else, and the only criteria for my behavior will be what works to accomplish my desires.

There are, of course, external factors that condition our behavior. Appropriate structures of financial accountability may prevent us from stealing from the company. The threat of an audit may keep us from cheating on our taxes. The fear of AIDS may restrain some people from practicing sexual promiscuity. Most of us will not commit a crime that will land us in jail or take some action that will embarrass our family or friends—though given the right circumstances, all of us may be capable of it. External restraints can condition our behavior from the outside in. But the first lesson we learned from David's story is that "God looks on the heart." Spirituality has to do with the way we live from the inside out. It is about the degree to which we practice the presence of God in the inner depths of our souls so that God's will begins to shape our actions from the inside out.

For most of us most of the time, the story will not be as disastrous or as colorful as it was for David. It happened for me in a much more mundane (i.e., ordinary, routine, humdrum) way while I was attempting to complete this book.

In recent years I have been growing in my own experience of what it means to live from the inside out. I've been moving toward a life that is intentionally centered in God and rooted in prayer. I can tell the difference between days that begin with my quiet time of meditation on scripture and prayerful reflection—what E. Stanley Jones called his "listening post"—and those days when I rush into action on my own without centering myself in the action of God. On this particular day, I woke up early and went straight to my computer. While it was booting up, I put on the coffee and dove into the work. Several hours later I could feel an increase of internal stress. My mind was scattered; my attention distracted. There were words on the screen, but they didn't march in any coherent direction.

Around midday, I stopped typing. I realized that I had not begun the day with the discipline of prayer that centers my activity in the activity of God's Spirit. It was as if I expected to complete the work myself, under my own power, with my own creativity. I left the computer and went out on the porch of the Great Smoky Mountain cabin where I was writing. I sat down in a wooden rocker. I listened to the sound of the rushing creek. I took time to feel the cool mountain breeze on my face. I watched the sunlight splatter through the trees. I read the psalm for the day and focused my attention on the words of scripture. I concentrated my attention away from myself and onto the presence of God. My chaotic spirit began to be at rest. In that quiet, sacred space of the soul, I began to feel the inner peace that comes from allowing the Spirit of God to order our thoughts and direct our actions. I returned to my work with a deep sense that I was not alone, but that my mind and heart and soul were in harmony with the creative Spirit of God.

I heard a radio preacher declare that our prayers "move the hand of God." He talked about it the way a mechanic would describe the way the transmission controls the speed of your car. The preacher said that we make things happen in this world by the way we pray. I'm not sure about that. Although I have deep confidence in the amazing way God's power is released into our lives through prayer, this particular preacher's approach was a little too tightly focused on what *we* do to influence God, as if *we* are in control. The primary focus of spiritual discipline is not my desire to "move the hands of God" or to get God to do what I'd like to see happen, but rather on bringing my life into harmony with the movement of God.

Prayer is the process by which I keep my life in gear with the Spirit of God, who is already at work to accomplish God's loving, redeeming purpose in this world. The purpose of prayer is not to convince a sometimes reluctant God to act on my behalf, but to break through my reluctance so God can reorder my desires, redirect my energies, and remold my actions in the likeness of Jesus Christ. Prayer is the discipline of spiritual fitness that strengthens my soul, just the way the disciplines of physical fitness strengthen my body.

Don Shelby is a writer, preacher, and pastor in California. I feel the force of his description of the discipline of prayer:

> Prayer is not only quiet contemplation, it is also hard work. It is not only folded hands, it is also bruised knuckles knocking in the dark. It is not only a joyful finding, it also can be perennial seeking. It is not only a humble receiving, it is also audacious asking. Prayer is not always like a cloister; it more often is like a workout gym, a rehearsal hall, or a batter's box. . . . A weekend golfer sometimes gets off a great shot, a passenger assisted through radio instructions can land an airplane in an emergency, an amateur writer sometimes turns an unforgettable phrase. But to win the British open, to command a transcontinental jetliner, or to garner the Nobel Prize in literature takes more than an occasional experience and natural ability. It requires natural ability and practice; dedication and practice, inspiration and practice . . . the regimen of conditioning and the grueling routine of practice day after day. (Sermon, "Making Prayer Work," July 24, 1983)

A concert pianist said that if he missed his practice session for one day, he knew it. If he missed practice for two days, his teacher knew it. If he failed to practice for three days, his wife knew it. And if he missed his practice time at the keyboard for four days or more, everyone knew it. It doesn't take that many days for me! If I miss my quiet time with God for one day, I know it, my wife knows it, and there is a good chance that the church staff will know it. I can fake the love of God in my life for a little while, but this is generally like the manna that God provided for the children of Israel in the desert: it was only good for one day and turned rotten if the people tried to keep it for the next. They had to receive their sustenance fresh every morning.

David thought he was autonomous, that he was free to do whatever it took to get whatever he wanted. Rather than allowing his actions to be shaped by a life-giving attraction to God, he gave himself to the fatal attraction of his own self-satisfying desires. That's the meaning of sin, and it always leads to death. God, who had been so noticeably left out of this chapter, shows up in the final, ominous sentence: "But the thing that David had done displeased the LORD" (2 Samuel 11:27b).

> Give ear to my words, O LORD;
>   give heed to my sighing.
> Listen to the sound of my cry,
>   my King and my God,
>   for to you I pray.
> O LORD, in the morning you hear my voice;
>   in the morning I plead my case to you, and watch.
>
> For you are not a God who delights in wickedness;
>   evil will not sojourn with you.
> The boastful will not stand before your eyes;
>   you hate all evildoers.
> You destroy those who speak lies;
>   the LORD abhors the bloodthirsty and deceitful.
>
> But I, through the abundance of your steadfast love,
>   will enter your house,
> I will bow down toward your holy temple
>   in awe of you.
> Lead me, O LORD, in your righteousness
>   because of my enemies;
> make your way straight before me.
>
>   (Psalm 5:1-8)

Time Out

As I worked on this chapter, I found myself moving in the direction of prevention rather than cure. How can we develop the kind of living relationship with God that will prevent us from falling into the temptations of power that caught David? What kind of spiritual fitness program will strengthen us to face temptation? How can we develop a life of prayer that will keep the power and presence of God as a living force within us? Given what we see in David's life, the answer to those questions may mean the difference between life and death.

As simply and as directly as possible, let me offer six practical elements for effective prayer. These are drawn from the teachings on prayer in the New Testament epistle of James. Reflect on these by yourself and/or discuss them with a group.

1. Confession: *Get real and get right with God.* Who do you think you are trying to impress? "Confess your sins to one another. . . . The prayer of the righteous is powerful and effective" (James 5:16).

2. Connection: *Get rooted in scripture.* What other source book do you have? "Take the prophets who spoke in the name of the Lord" (James 5:10).

3. Communication: *Get simple.* What makes you think you have to sound like Shakespeare? "Let your 'Yes' be yes and your 'No' be no" (James 5:12).

4. Consistency: *Get with it.* Why do you think spiritual maturity is a short-term project? "You also must be patient. Strengthen your hearts" (James 5: 8). "Let endurance have its full effect, so that you may

be mature and complete, lacking in nothing" (James 1:4).

5. Community: *Get some help.* Why are you trying to do this on your own? "Call for the elders of the church. . . . Pray for one another, so that you may be healed" (James 5:14-16).

6. Concentration: *Get focused on God's will.* Who's really in charge around here? "You ought to say, 'If the Lord wishes, we will live and do this'" (James 4:15).

7. *Prayer:*

Stupendous love of God most high!
He comes to meet us from the sky
   In mildest majesty,
Full of unutterable grace,
He calls the weary burden'd race,
   "Come all for help to me."

Tired with the greatness of my way,
From him I would no longer stray,
   But rest in Jesus have;
Weary of sin, from sin would cease,
Weary of mine own righteousness,
   And stoop, myself to save.

Weary of passions unsubdued,
Weary of vows in vain renew'd,
   Of forms without the power,
Of prayers, and hopes, complaints, and groans,
My fainting soul in silence owns
   I can hold out no more.

. . . .

Mine utter helplessness I feel;
But thou, who gav'st the feeble will,
   The effectual grace supply:

S

I

N

Be thou my strength, my light, my way,
And bid my soul the call obey,
   And to thy bosom fly.

Fulfil thine own intense desire,
And now into my heart inspire
   The power of faith and love;
Then, Saviour, then to thee I come,
And find on earth the life, the home,
   The rest of saints above.

Charles Wesley

Chapter Ten

Choices

The Tangled Web We Weave

2 Samuel 12:1-25

Oh, what a tangled web we weave
When first we practice to deceive.

—*Sir Walter Scott*

If my memory is correct, it was Daniel Patrick Moynihan who captured the mood of my generation in the aftermath of President John F. Kennedy's assassination when he said that we would laugh again, but we would never be young again. That's the truth about the way life goes on after a great tragedy, in the wake of some major loss, in the aftermath of moral failure. The healing, forgiving, relentless grace of God enables us to laugh again, live again, and love again, but we can never be young again. Life is never quite the same.

I was completing work on this book in August 1998 when President Clinton delivered his four-minute "confession" in which he acknowledged that he had had an "inappropriate relationship" with Monica Lewinsky and that he "misled" his family, friends, and the American people. In reflecting on it with my church members on the Internet, I compared the Clinton story to a tragedy by Shakespeare or a novel by Faulkner in which a person with great talent and the opportunity to accomplish great good squanders it all in a self-destructive pattern that plays directly into the political viciousness and moral carelessness around him. One thing we knew for sure: Things would never be the same again. Dag Hammarskjöld described the ongoing consequences of our choices when he wrote:

So, once again, you chose for yourself—and opened the door to chaos. The chaos you become whenever God's hand does not rest upon your head.

He who has once been under God's hand, has lost his innocence: only he feels the full explosive force of destruction which is released by a moment's surrender to temptation. (*Markings*, p. 104)

That's the truth about David's life after the Bathsheba-Uriah debacle. By the grace of God, David is forgiven. He goes on living; he continues to be king. But things are never the same. In fact, things get downright messy from here on. You can feel it in the biblical text. The early stories of David's life are simple and clear. They are told in crisp, colorful language so that even a child can repeat them. But after 2 Samuel 11, the narrative becomes tangled and complex. Your kids couldn't follow the story if you wanted them to. It's not easy to sort through the tangled web of deceit, rape, murder, political intrigue, and national conflict that clutters the remainder of David's reign.

Biblical scholars call these passages the "succession narratives." The die has been cast. From here on the story is not so much about David as it is about the twisted process by which his successor is chosen. It's not that God has given up on David. God is still faithful to the purpose that had been at work in David's life since adolescence. But in the aftermath of the king's midlife fling with sexual passion and deceitful power, that purpose must be worked out in the dysfunctional network of bruised and broken lives that are the product of David's arrogant attempt to live without God. It's not a pretty path we follow from here on, but it leads into deep places in a man's soul. It tracks the journey of every person who attempts to live autonomously, without the presence and power of God, which I assume includes, to one degree or another, just about every one of us.

Like most of us some of the time and some of us most of the time, David wanted to avoid the consequences of his choices. When we left him at the end of the last episode, it appeared as if he might get away with it, too. He had covered his tracks about as well as one man could. But then we heard this ominous word: "But the thing that David had done displeased the LORD" (2 Samuel 11:27*b*). Though David acted as if God was not around, this did not mean that God had gone off to Walt Disney World for a vacation. Martin Luther King, Jr., often quoted the words of James Russell Lowell:

Though the cause of evil prosper,
    Yet 'tis truth alone is strong;
Though her portion be the scaffold,
    And upon the throne be wrong:
Yet that scaffold sways the future,
    And, behind the dim unknown,
Standeth God within the shadow
    keeping watch above his own.
("Once to Every Man and Nation")

Bette Midler reminded us of the same thing in her hit song, "God is watching us / from a distance." Having been effectively left out of the last episode, the word of God now enters the story in the form of a prophet named Nathan (2 Samuel 11:27–12:1).

Let's get one thing straight: Biblical prophets are not palm-reading fortunetellers. Biblical prophets are God-centered people who speak the truth when falsehood has become believable. They are like the little kid who pointed out that the emperor had no clothes, when everyone else in the empire was afraid to state the obvious. The prophets announce the future effect of present actions. Prophets remind us of the long-term consequences of short-term choices. They are faithful people who won't let us off the hook of responsibility for our actions.

I am grateful for the prophets in my life. Some of them are the clergy cronies in my retreat group. Some are colleagues on my church staff. Some are brothers and sisters within my congregation. One of them is my wife. Two of them are my daughters. They are Spirit-sensitive people whose presence in my life is a constant reminder of my accountability before God and the effect my choices have on others. Without them, I could be capable of the same kind of fatal attraction to selfish ambition that infected David. With them, I am strengthened, encouraged, supported, and confirmed in my desire to be a faithful disciple of Jesus Christ.

In 1979 I was appointed to a vacant palmetto field on the edge of Walt Disney World and given the task of birthing a new congregation. When I asked for advice from Walter Rutland, who has been one of the personal prophets in my life, he immediately replied, "Don't be overly impressed with small successes or overly discouraged by major defeats." Across the next thirteen years, there would be plenty of small successes and major defeats, but Walter Rutland taught me to keep my eye on the long-term goal and to measure the way immediate choices would either move us toward that goal or away from it. His words continue to be a prophetic guide for my ministry today.

The prophet Nathan was no dummy. He had been around David's court long enough to know that the direct approach would be met with big-time royal defensiveness. So, he told David a parable—the way Jesus told parables—to allow the unpleasant truth to take him by surprise. Nathan told a parable about a very rich man who had plenty of flocks and a poor man who only had one small lamb. In spite of his wealth, the rich man took the poor man's lamb and served up lamb chops to his guest for dinner (2 Samuel 12:1-4).

The parable worked. Nathan had hardly finished the tale before the injustice of it sank into David's soul. David had, after all, lived with God. Behind his arrogance, David was still a man with a divinely conditioned conscience. He was still capable of moral outrage. "David's anger was greatly kindled against the man" (2 Samuel 12:5). Then the prophet declared the ringing words of judgment to the king: "You are the man!" (v. 7).

Those moments come to all of us. One of them came to the president of the United States when the sordid details of his sexual behavior and dishonesty became public knowledge. These are awesome moments of self-awareness, when we are forced to face up to who we are; moments of absolute honesty, when we see how we have "gone down" on our deepest convictions and highest values; defining moments in which we acknowledge that we are not the "masters of our universe" after all.

Sometimes the truth comes to us through another person, the way it came to David through Nathan. That's how it came to a fellow pastor who was confronted with the painful truth of his failure by a friend who loved him enough to speak the truth when everyone else was in denial.

Sometimes we face reality because of a growing internal discomfort with the way we are living. That's how it happened for a man who finally shared with me the inner conflict he was experiencing because of a long-term adulterous relationship.

Sometimes we are forced to face ourselves through crisis. That's the way the truth came to a friend who suddenly found himself facing legal charges for inappropriate financial dealings in which he had been involved.

Sometimes the truth makes itself known through our physical body, the way it happened with a friend whose ethical conflict produced an ulcer that could have taken his life.

However it comes, we know that the finger of truth is pointed in our direction. We hear the Spirit of God saying, "You are the man."

As Nathan reminded King David of everything God had done for him, David realized how he had squandered God's goodness, broken God's trust, abused God's love, and rejected God's will. He wrapped it all up in one powerful confession: "I have sinned against the LORD" (2 Samuel 12:13). The most eloquent commentary on that confession came from David himself. The traditional Hebrew text identifies Psalm 51 as "A Psalm of David, when the prophet Nathan came to him, after he had gone in to Bathsheba."

> Have mercy on me, O God,
>   according to your steadfast love;
> according to your abundant mercy
>   blot out my transgressions.
> Wash me thoroughly from my iniquity,
>   and cleanse me from my sin.
>
> For I know my transgressions,
>   and my sin is ever before me.
> Against you, you alone, have I sinned,
>   and done what is evil in your sight.
> . . . .
> You desire truth in the inward being;
>   therefore teach me wisdom in my secret heart.
> Purge me with hyssop, and I shall be clean;
>   wash me, and I shall be whiter than snow.
> Let me hear joy and gladness;
>   let the bones that you have crushed rejoice.
> Hide your face from my sins,
>   and blot out all my iniquities.
>
> Create in me a clean heart, O God,
>   and put a new and right spirit within me.
> Do not cast me away from your presence,
>   and do not take your holy spirit from me.
> Restore to me the joy of your salvation,
>   and sustain in me a willing spirit.
>   (verses 1-4a, 6-12)

Those are the words of a man who has faced the reality of his sin and who is on the way to forgiveness. And here's the amazing, grace-filled part: *God forgave David!* In fact, Nathan made it sound as if God's forgiveness was retroactive: "The LORD has put away your sin" (2 Samuel 12:13*b*). God's forgiveness was ready and waiting for David the moment he was ready to receive it. God's grace is always prior to our repentance and greater than our sin. David is forgiven! His relationship with God is restored. But David's life will never be the same.

Nathan points to the consequences of David's actions: "Now therefore the sword shall never depart from your house" (2 Samuel 12:10). David's violence gives rise to more violence. David's arrogant attempt to live with accountability to nothing but his own power, lust, and greed is passed on like a genetic flaw to his children. The child born of David's lust dies in infancy (2 Samuel 12:15*b*-23). Amnon, son of David and heir to the throne, rapes his half-sister, Tamar, and is killed in vengeance by her brother Absalom (2 Samuel 13). Absalom, the fair-haired son whom David loved and the crowds adored, leads a rebellion against his father and dies in the battle (2 Samuel 14–18). Because of all the blood on his hands, David is not permitted to fulfill his dream of building the Temple (1 Chronicles 22:6-10). David was forgiven, sure enough, but the toxic effects of his actions would continue to disrupt his family for years to come.

The story of David is a painful drama. It is not unlike the lesson in an episode of *The Andy Griffith Show* where young Opie has killed a bird with his brand new slingshot. Opie asks Andy, his pa, "You gonna give me a whippin'?" Andy replies, "Nope, I'm not gonna give you a whippin'." Andy opens the window. "You hear that?" he asks Opie. "That's those young birds chirpin' for their mama that's never comin' back. Now you just listen to that for a while." Look at David's life, listen to the cry of pain that echoes through his children, and you will begin to feel the heart-wrenching consequences of his choices.

The Hebrew writers were looking back on David's life as historians when they put these stories together. They were trying to answer very practical questions. What caused a man who began so well to end up with so much turmoil, conflict, and disappointment? Why did he do what he did? That's what historians do: they try to figure out where things went wrong.

On the surface, the answer seems simple enough. The historians might say that it all started one spring day when most kings go to war; but this king, on this day, went to bed with a woman named Bathsheba. Human actions have human consequences. We reap what we sow. We are free to choose our actions, but we are not free to choose the consequences of those actions. We are not islands to ourselves; we are part of an interwoven web of life. That's where both King David and President Clinton got it wrong. Matters of truth and sexuality are not ultimately private matters; they are inextricably woven into the fabric of human relationships. We are not our own; this is the lie of an overly individualized, self-absorbed culture.

But David's story is not just human history; this is *sacred* history. The biblical writers were not only looking at David's actions; they were looking for *God's* action. They wrote the story this way to demonstrate that our lives, our history, and our world are under the influence of a just and righteous God. If we choose to break God's laws, the effects ripple through our own lives and the lives of others. God has written cause and effect into the life of the universe. If you break the moral law of God, you will pay for it, or worse, some innocent person may feel the effects of your sin.

Sometimes I think the biblical historians got it right. Our actions do have uncontrollable and incalculable effects on others around us. I recently read of a concept in astrophysics known as "the butterfly effect." Simply put, it says that if a butterfly on earth flaps its wings, the effect can be felt in galaxies thousands of light years away. I can't prove that this is true for butterflies, but I know it is true in human relationships. We cannot ultimately "do our own thing," because whatever we do affects someone else.

Take war, for instance. When nations go to war there are always unforeseen, indirect consequences that visit the innocent in the second and third generations. Just because we "win" the war doesn't mean that we won't experience the consequences.

There's a grave in a hillside cemetery in a small town in Western Pennsylvania where my grandparents buried their infant son. He was among the 200,000 Americans who died in the flu epidemic of 1918. I had seen the grave many times; I had heard the stories about Harold's death. But I was reading a book on the AIDS epidemic when I realized that the flu epidemic in which infant Harold died was a direct result of massive movements of people in World War I. The author also asserted that the widespread outbreak of polio in the late 1940s and early 1950s was a direct result of what he called the "viral mixing bowl" of the world wars. Harold's death was one of the unintended consequences of war.

I know that the principle of unintended consequences is true, but I also know that it is not the whole story. Hindsight is always 20/20. Historians always have the advantage of looking into the maze from above, rather than being caught within it. Sometimes the connections are not that simple. Sometimes causes and effects are clearly and closely related, but sometimes they aren't. Our lives are affected by an infinite array of stimuli from a wide array of sources. Sometimes a person apparently does everything right, but everything goes wrong. And sometimes some jerk does everything wrong but it all seems to come out right. I've seen the sins of the fathers visited on the second and third generations, but I've also seen it the other way around, too; I've seen the sins of the children visited on their parents. I've heard the cries of conscientious, loving, responsible parents, who ask, "What did we do wrong?" And I've found myself responding, "You probably didn't do anything wrong. You can't take responsibility for every stupid choice your son or daughter made. You weren't the only influence in their lives."

Although we are inexorably bound together in a tangled web of human relationships, we are not prisoners of fate within that web. We are influenced by our past, but we are not bound by it. Although we stand before the justice of God being worked out in human history, we also receive the gifts of God's unexpected mercy. Just as I have seen God's judgment at work in the consequences of human choices, I have also seen God's grace pick up the broken pieces of a person's life and put them together in new and amazing ways. There's mystery in this life. It's not as fatalistic as we might be led to think. We never see every piece of the story, and we must always be on the lookout for the surprising grace of God. Don't miss those beautiful verses in the aftermath of the death of Bathsheba's first child:

> Then David comforted his wife Bathsheba. He had intercourse with her, and she bore a son, whom David named Solomon. The LORD loved the boy and commanded the prophet Nathan to name the boy Jedidiah ["Beloved of the LORD"], because the LORD loved him. (2 Samuel 12:24-25 TEV)

Who would have predicted that the same union that caused such turmoil and pain would also give birth to Solomon? Who would have guessed that the tangled mess of David's dysfunctional family would also produce the king who would become known as the wisest man who ever lived? Who would have predicted that the same bed that gave birth to sorrow and pain would also give birth to this gift of hope, "the beloved of God"? And who would have predicted that when Matthew listed the genealogy of Jesus, he would include "the wife of Uriah" in the line of God's covenant (Matthew 1:6)? God has an amazing way of creating new life out of the shattered pieces of our past. Playwright Eugene O'Neil described it in these wonderful lines from "The Great God Brown":

> "This is Daddy's bedtime secret for today: Man is born broken. He lives by mending. The grace of God is glue!" (Act 4, Scene 1)

A contemporary gospel song captures this same word of hope in a beautiful way:

> Something beautiful, something good;
> all my confusion he understood;
> all I had to offer him was brokenness and strife,
> but he made something beautiful of my life.
> (Gloria Gaither, "Something Beautiful")

In the constant crucible of the choices we make, David's story would urge us to remember the butterfly effect. Remember the tangled web we weave. Remember that once the action is taken, the consequences may be uncontrollable and things will never be the same. Remember that God is not an absentee landlord; God is still with us, even when we think we are on our own. God is not just watching us from a distance; God is actively and intimately involved in the ordinary patterns of our human existence. For the sake of all those whom our actions will affect, David's story challenges us to develop deep sensitivity to God's guidance and close relationships for spiritual accountability.

But to the person who is struggling under the effects of someone else's foolish actions or the person who is bearing the weight of damaged emotions and broken relationships in the past, David's story offers a hope-filled reminder of the grace of God. Remember that

God isn't finished with you yet. God's grace is not bounded by the limitations of human cause and effect. The unexpected mercy and grace of God can surprise you with new gifts of life and hope. Who knows? Just when everything seems to be coming apart at the seams, there may be a Solomon waiting to be born.

> Make me to know your ways, O LORD;
>   teach me your paths.
> Lead me in your truth, and teach me,
>   for you are the God of my salvation;
> for you I wait all day long.
>
> Be mindful of your mercy, O LORD, and of your steadfast love,
>   for they have been from of old.
> Do not remember the sins of my youth or my transgressions;
>   according to your steadfast love remember me,
> for your goodness' sake, O LORD!
>
> Good and upright is the LORD;
>   therefore he instructs sinners in the way.
> He leads the humble in what is right,
>   and teaches the humble his way.
> All the paths of the LORD are steadfast love and faithfulness,
>   for those who keep his covenant and his decrees.
>
> For your name's sake, O LORD,
>   pardon my guilt, for it is great.
> . . . .
> My eyes are ever toward the LORD,
>   for he will pluck my feet out of the net.
>
> Turn to me and be gracious to me,
>   for I am lonely and afflicted.
> Relieve the troubles of my heart,
>   and bring me out of my distress.
> Consider my affliction and my trouble,
>   and forgive all my sins.
> (Psalm 25:4-11, 15-18)

Time Out

1. *The president's confession.* The first draft of this book was completed shortly after President Clinton acknowledged an "inappropriate relationship" with a White House intern. A physician/friend/former tennis buddy/Notre Dame grad sent his reflections on the story to me via the Internet:

> I think the men of our generation will use [President Clinton's] example as a way of looking at our lives and searching for the decency within. His unfortunate example of a life unexamined will in a funny way propel many men to look anew at their own lives. Are we, at our core, decent men? Do we behave in a truthful, simple, inner-directed fashion? What really matters? Is it personal gain and aggrandizement or is it the basic, honest, human interactions between people? Are we honest with others in our lives? Do we speak directly about our lives, our feelings, our needs, and our fears or do we continue to obfuscate and let others see only our "false selves"? Maybe more men will begin to see the type of man they don't want to be. As St. Francis Xavier said: What does it profit a man to gain the world, yet lose his soul?

I could not help pointing out to my Notre Dame friend that if St. Francis Xavier said that, he was quoting Jesus! My friend went on to write:

> It is interesting how life's twists and turns do bring us face to face with certain walls we have to learn to deal with or learn from. I do think this country is on the brink of a new awakening. I think men are more free to be themselves, to express themselves and abandon old roles that they used to wear like armor. I certainly hope so.

C
H
O
I
C
E
S

What a tragedy a man can get to that point in his life, and attain so much power and position, and yet attain so little insight about himself and his own humanness. That is the biggest tragedy of all: what appears to be an inability to be truly humble or at least a willingness to humble oneself in the face of one's very human mistakes. What a great lesson for all our children and our peers if he could have asked for forgiveness and been truly contrite. That would have been an extraordinary healing and human experience.

How did *you* respond to President Clinton's confession from the inside out? Can you identify with the questions it raised for my friend in his own spiritual growth? In what ways?

2. *Listen for the prophet.* Who are the prophets in your life? Who are the people who provide loving, honest, clear accountability for you? How do they accomplish this?

3. *Facing the consequences.* How have you seen the painful consequences of human choices being worked out in your experience? How have you experienced the surprising gifts of God's grace?

4. *Finding forgiveness.* Read Psalm 51. Allow the words to settle into your soul. Think about and try to feel the process that was going on in David's life when he first spoke them. When have you felt that kind of guilt? Where can you identify with David's longing for mercy? When have you wanted to be made clean? How have you experienced the forgiveness David describes?

5. *Prayer.*

Come, O thou all-victorious Lord!
Thy power to us make known;

Strike with the hammer of thy word,
    And break these hearts of stone.

O that we all might now begin
    Our foolishness to mourn;
And turn at once from every sin,
    And to our Saviour turn!

Give us ourselves and thee to know,
    In this our gracious day;
Repentance unto life bestow,
    And take our sins away.

Conclude us first in unbelief,
    And freely then release;
Fill every soul with sacred grief,
    And then with sacred peace.

Impoverish, Lord, and then relieve,
    And then enrich the poor;
The knowledge of our sickness give,
    The knowledge of our cure.

That blessed sense of guilt impart,
    And then remove the load;
Trouble, and wash the troubled heart
    In the atoning blood.

Our desperate state through sin declare,
    And speak our sins forgiven;
By perfect holiness prepare,
    And take us up to heaven.

                    Charles Wesley

Chapter Eleven

Fathering

What Will We Leave the Kids?

1 Chronicles 22:6-19

> If I were given the opportunity to present a gift to the next
> generation, it would be the ability for each
> individual to laugh at himself.
>
> —*Charles Schulz*

What will we leave the kids?" The answer
to that question involves more than financial estate planning. Asking
that question can help us get a handle on one of the most important
tasks to which every man is called, namely, the task of "fathering."

By "fathering" I'm describing more than the biological process of
conceiving (which is generally fun!), birthing (which is downright
amazing!), and raising (which is always a challenge!) our genetic offspring. Though I highly recommend the process as one of God's great
adventures for a man's life, I want to stretch our concept of "fathering"
to describe our common calling to pass on spiritual values to the next
generation. Some men fulfill that calling with children by birth or
adoption in their human families. Some fulfill it with children in the
family of faith. All of us bear responsibility for the values we pass on
to children in our culture. The critical question for every member of
Sam Keen's Society for the Protection and Encouragement of
Righteous Manhood (SPERM) is not so much what we will pass on
from the *outside* in terms of wealth or genetics, but what we will pass
on from the *inside* in terms of our spiritual values and faith.

We have a pickup truck–load of good reasons to be concerned about
the values boys are inheriting in this culture. Here's one tragic example: it seems that every time you turn around, there's been another in

the tragic string of school shootings somewhere across the country. I don't think it is a coincidence that in every case, the gun that did the killing was in the hand of a boy. One report focusing on the boys who committed these crimes noted, "Boys everywhere are frustrated, abused, and saturated with media violence" in America (*Time*, July 6, 1998; p. 58). Of course, the boys who pulled these triggers are exceptional cases, but we would be foolish not to see their tragic stories as warning signs of ominous trends. They may be like the canary that miners once carried into the mine shaft as a test for inadequate oxygen. When the canary stopped singing, it was the warning sign for the miners to get to better air. The evidence is that it is high time we got serious about the task of spiritual fathering. What kind of spiritual inheritance are we leaving for our kids?

In one sense, King David isn't much help on this one. He was a lousy father. To call his family dysfunctional would be a high compliment. The sordid tale of Amnon's rape of Tamar (2 Samuel 13) is a case study in sexual abuse followed by paternal denial. David's conflict with Absalom (see 2 Samuel 14–15, 18) is the tragic portrayal of parental inconsistency and competition for power. The struggle between Adonijah and Solomon for succession to the throne (1 Kings 1) is a soap opera of trickery and deceit, with Solomon's mother, Bathsheba, and the prophet Nathan thrown into the mix. It's all very messy stuff.

From a family systems perspective, you could say David was functioning out of what he had inherited. His father, Jesse, had all but forgotten that he existed. His sibling relationships were infected with jealousy and competition. Saul, the man who became his paternal role model, tried to kill him. It would be enough stuff to keep a professional psychologist in business for years! At the least, David proves that it's tough to be a good father if you haven't experienced having one.

But the biblical narrative is more than the historical account of a dysfunctional royal family. This is the story of the relentlessly faithful God who works through the chaos of human choices to accomplish the purpose of steadfast love. God is faithful, and at the end, David got it together well enough to pass on some good gifts to Solomon. A cynic might say that David waited too long to atone, that he was merely trying to reshape his legacy, or that his actions and their timing were sort of like cramming for a final exam. A more generous reading could be that David had finally learned the lesson of all the pathos and tragedy of his life. Some would suggest that Davidic spinmeisters were improving the record for scripture. Some or all of those very human factors may be present in the text, but beneath it all is the presence of the God who promised steadfast love (*hesed*) to David's house and brought a gift of hope for the future out of the chaos David's failures had created. By the time David was ready to pass on the kingdom to Solomon, God had given him a gift of spiritual insight that may provide practical guidance for all of us as we search for more effective fathering. It is the kind of spiritual inheritance that could make a radical difference for our sons and daughters. First, David left Solomon a sense of calling: "Then [David] called for his son Solomon and charged him to build a house for the LORD, the God of Israel" (1 Chronicles 22:6).

David's bequest to Solomon is set in the context of the greatest construction project in biblical history. David's last royal act was to purchase the site, design the plans, and gather the materials for a Temple he would not live to see completed. Don't miss the spiritual principle at work here. The writer of the letter to the Hebrews described people who lived by faith as those who "died in faith without having received the promises, but from a distance they saw and greeted them" (Hebrews 11:13). Biblical faith always means committing ourselves to something bigger and larger than our own lives, namely, the Kingdom, the rule and will of God, which is being fulfilled in human history. In the same sense, we need to pass on to our children a sense of calling to a task that is larger than their own self-interest. We need to help them discover their connection with something that is bigger than their own needs and desires; something that will outlive and outlast their lifetime.

A Franciscan priest named Richard Rohr spent five years studying cultural initiation rites for guiding boys into manhood. He found that a common element in those rites of passage is the realization for the boy that his life is not his own. The son learns that life is not just about his interests, but that his life is set inside "a sacred universe of meaning . . . the young man knows in his very bones that '*my life is not about* me' " (*Sojourners*, May–June 1998, p. 18; italics his).

To know that "my life is not about me" is to feel that I am part of a larger web of relationships with my human family, my community, and my world. Spiritually, it means learning that life is about finding my unique place in the fulfillment of God's loving purpose for the whole creation. If we can pass the gift of that knowledge on to our children, it will be a radical contradiction of the values they are inheriting from the contemporary culture.

While every sports fan's eyes were glued to the 1998 NBA finals to see if the Chicago Bulls could do it again (they did!), the cover of *Sports Illustrated* asked, "Where's Daddy?" A special report looked at the disturbing pattern of star athletes fathering children with little or no sense of responsibility for the legal, financial, and emotional consequences. *SI*'s "NBA All-Paternity Team" of players who have conceived children out of wedlock included many of the big names in professional basketball. Len Elmore, former NBA player and current ESPN broadcaster, quit working as an agent in part because of "a lack of responsibility" among the players. When asked what would account for such irresponsible behavior by individual players, Elmore said, "Today's athletes don't care. . . . They're hung up on instant gratification. There's no view of the impact that present-day decisions have on the future" (*Sports Illustrated*, May 4, 1998; p. 69).

It's not just the NBA. Our sons and daughters are growing up in a culture that hinges on instant gratification with very little regard for the long-term consequences of present choices. In one of the most popular shows on television, the managing partner of a successful law firm declared that they operated on the basis of "selfism," which he said meant that when all of them are out for themselves, all of them make a profit. By contrast, one of the most revolutionary gifts we can leave our children is a deep, inner awareness that "my life is not about me."

I am grateful for a father who gave me that gift. Everyone knew Dad was a workaholic and that most of his life's energy went into building his business. But everyone who knew him across the years of his life in that small Western Pennsylvania town—one of those towns where everyone seemed to know everything about everyone else— knew that there was more to his life than that. Deeper than his commitment to his business was his commitment to Jesus Christ.

They knew it by the way he never missed worship and Sunday school on Sunday morning. They heard it in the way he always told the truth and never made a dishonest deal. Some of them experienced it in the way he gave them a job when no one else would take a risk on them, or the way he carried their credit until they could pay their bills. They felt it when they called on him to pray—the one guy in the crowd who would pray in public. They could see it in the way he loved his wife and his sons and the way he respected his father. They would have understood it if they had known his practice of the biblical discipline of tithing, giving the first 10 percent of his income for God's work in this world. And they saw it in the way he faced death from cancer at the age of fifty-nine. He was far too young to die, but he prepared for his death with an inner peace born out of his confidence in the hope of eternal life. He modeled a life of faith and encouraged me to listen for God's call. Even when that calling took me far away from his home, he encouraged me to follow wherever it would lead. He taught me that my life is not about me but is about following the will of God.

David's second bequest to Solomon, and the second gift we need to pass on to our children, is the challenge to be men of peace.

> David said to Solomon, "My son, I had planned to build a house to the name of the LORD my God. But the word of the LORD came to me, saying, 'You have shed much blood and have waged great wars; you shall not build a house to my name, because you have shed so much blood in my sight on the earth. See, a son shall be born to you; he shall be a man of peace. I will give him peace from all his enemies on every side; for his name shall be Solomon, and I will give peace and quiet to Israel in his days. He shall build a house for my name. He shall be a son to me, and I will be a father to him, and I will establish his royal throne in Israel forever.' " (1 Chronicles 22:7-10)

The reason David was not permitted to build the Temple was not that he lacked the resources, workers, money, or plans. It was that he had shed so much blood; his life had been filled with so much violence. Is it possible that the primary reason we seem to be so incapable of building the kind of families, communities, nation, and world we would like to build is that we are up to our knees in blood?

Manhood in our culture is soaked with violence. From early childhood, boys are taught that the way to prove their manhood is to fight, control, dominate, and win at all costs. The cartoons they watch on Saturday morning, the games they play on the computer, the movies they see in the theater, the toys they get with their fast-food hamburgers, the wars they see their fathers and grandfathers fight; these and a thousand other stimuli condition them to believe that a man who is not violent is a "wimp," a "sissy," or worse. As they move into adolescence, they learn that sex is about conquest, scoring, getting and taking, domination and control. After saturating them with so much internal and external violence, why should we be surprised if they act in ways that are consistent with what they have learned? It reminds me of the Alcoholics Anonymous principle that insanity is doing the same thing over and over and expecting different results.

Perhaps David had experienced enough violence. Perhaps he had seen enough bloodshed. Perhaps he had learned that the only man God can use to fulfill God's vision, the only man who can genuinely be called God's son, is the man of peace and nonviolence. Jesus, the "son of David," tried to teach us the same lesson.

Would you like to know the most consistently neglected teaching of Jesus? Would you like to read the words that faithful people across two thousand years of Christian tradition have steadfastly ignored, neglected, or interpreted in ways that contradict what Jesus said? Would you like to know the words of scripture that even the most literal-minded Christians consistently refuse to take literally? Here they are:

> "Blessed are the peacemakers, for they will be called children of God." (Matthew 5:9)

> "You have heard that it was said, 'An eye for an eye and a tooth for a tooth.' But I say to you, . . . if anyone strikes you on the right cheek, turn the other also. (Matthew 5:38-39)

> "You have heard that it was said, 'You shall love your neighbor and hate your enemy." But I say to you, Love your enemies and pray for those who persecute you, so that you may be children of your Father in heaven. (Matthew 5:43-45a)

Both David and Jesus named peacemaking as the identifying mark of those who are in a father-child relationship with God. Now and then we catch glimpses of manly nonviolence and courageous peacemaking. We saw it in Ghandi. We saw it in Martin Luther King, Jr. We see it in Desmond Tutu. But by and large, we have not been willing to learn the lesson of nonviolence and peacemaking as a way of life. The apostle Paul said that we reap what we sow (Galatians 6:7-9). In the Garden of Gethsemane, Jesus warned us that those who live by the sword, die by the sword (Matthew 26:52). Jesus would weep over today's newspaper headlines the way he wept over the city of Jerusalem, saying, "If they only knew the things that make for peace" (see Luke 19:41-42). If we want to leave good gifts for our children, it may be time for us to learn the lessons of nonviolence and peace.

The third gift David bequeathed to Solomon, also one we need to pass on to our children, is wisdom.

> Now, my son, the LORD be with you, so that you may succeed in build-ing the house of the LORD your God, as he has spoken concerning you. Only, may the LORD grant you discretion and understanding, so that when he gives you charge over Israel you may keep the law of the LORD your God. Then you will prosper if you are careful to observe the statutes and the ordinances that the LORD commanded Moses for Israel. (1 Chronicles 22:11-13)

Biblical wisdom is not the accumulation of information; that's knowledge. Biblical wisdom is knowing what to do with the knowledge we acquire. Biblical wisdom is the presence of the Spirit of God giv-ing understanding and discernment so that we know how to live in the way and will of God. It's not enough just to "know" or quote the Bible. We need the gift of spiritual wisdom to translate the written word into a living Word in the very real situations we face.

Think back to your childhood. Did you ever talk back to your father? If you are a father, has your son or daughter ever talked back to you? The Bible says that if a son talks back to his father, he should be stoned (Leviticus 20:9). But generations of Spirit-led wisdom have taught people of faith to hold onto the value of parental respect but to give up the practice of stoning.

The Bible says, "Slaves, obey your earthly masters" (Ephesians 6:5). But across the generations, Spirit-empowered wisdom led faithful people to lead the abolition movement and to continue to work for freedom for oppressed people in this world.

The Bible says, "Wives, be subject to your husbands" (Ephesians 5:22). In our day, many faithful Christians lift that verse out of its con-text and use it to define a hierarchical structure of male authority in marriage. In doing so, they effectively ignore the biblical description of male domination as a part of the curse in the aftermath of sin (Genesis 3:16). They conveniently bypass the primary call of the apostle Paul to "be subject to one another out of reverence for Christ" (Ephesians 5:21). But Spirit-led wisdom across the generations has taught Christian people to shape marriage relationships in the love of Christ so that they do not become controlling, manipulative, or oppressive, but rather bring mutual joy to each partner. One of the great gifts men can give to their children is to model healthy, self-giving equality in their marriages.

It's not enough just to quote the Bible. The Bible itself says that the Spirit of wisdom must give understanding and discernment so that the written word becomes a living Word in our life. Paul prayed that his friends in Colossae would be "filled with the knowledge of God's will in all spiritual wisdom and understanding," to the end that they would "lead lives worthy of the Lord, fully pleasing to him" (Colossians 1:9-10).

People in the Methodist tradition have a particular way of searching for that wisdom. We say that scripture is primary. Everything must be held accountable to the authority of the Bible. Our first question is, What does the Bible say? There are three tools we use to interpret scripture. (1) We use *reason*: Does my reading of this text make sense? (2) We use *tradition*: What have Christian people across the centuries said about this text? (3) We use *experience*: How does this text help me understand my experience of God? The Wesleyan "quadrilateral" of scripture, interpreted by reason, tradition, and experience, has become a practical process in searching for the spiritual wisdom that can lead us in the way of truth.

Our sons and daughters are growing up in a culture in which knowledge is exploding and spirituality is rampant but biblical wisdom is rare. It is critically important that we model for them a biblically rooted, Christ-centered, Spirit-energized wisdom as we search for the will and purpose of God.

David's fourth bequest to Solomon came in the form of a direct command: "Be strong and of good courage. Do not be afraid or dismayed" (1 Chronicles 22:13). There's no wimpy, whining, plastic piety here. Paul prayed for that same strength to be at work in the lives of the Colossian Christians: "May you be made strong with all the strength that comes from [Christ's] glorious power, and may you be prepared to endure everything with patience, while joyfully giving thanks to [God]" (Colossians 1:11-12). A life of faith demands the kind of inner strength and personal courage that only the Spirit of God can give.

I've discovered that there is a gigantic difference between worldly bravado and biblical courage. Worldly bravado is the stuff we throw at others in order to protect ourselves. Worldly bravado is attempting to prove our manhood by pushing others away or putting others down. It's usually a sure sign of inner insecurity. Biblical courage comes from deep within the soul of a person who lives with a deep, rock-solid confidence in God. It is the kind of strength that enables a person to be faithful to God's purpose regardless of the odds.

I found a beautiful description of biblical courage in the autobiography of Nelson Mandela. The world stood in awe as we watched him emerge from nearly thirty years of political imprisonment to be elected the first President of the new South Africa. The question is often asked, How did he do it? After all those years in prison, all that suffering, all that injustice, how was he able to extend his hand to those who would have destroyed him? Where did that strength and courage come from? Here is his answer:

> The decades of oppression and brutality had another, unintended effect, and that was that it produced . . . men of such extraordinary courage, wisdom, and generosity that their like may never be known again. Perhaps it requires such depth of oppression to create such heights of character. . . .
>
> It is from these comrades in the struggle that I learned the meaning of courage. Time and again, I have seen men and women risk and give their lives for an idea. I have seen men stand up to attacks and torture without breaking, showing a strength and resiliency that defies the imagination. I learned that courage was not the absence of fear, but the triumph over it. (*Long Walk to Freedom,* Boston: Little, Brown, and Co., 1994, p. 542)

That's biblical courage: the kind of courage that comes from a deep, abiding confidence in the goodness of God. This kind of strength enables a person to hold on to what is right and to endure hardship with joy. The absolutely unique element in the strength for which Paul prays is that it prepares us to "endure everything with patience, while joyfully giving thanks to God."

I've watched all sorts of people endure all sorts of hardship. Some hold on with grit and grim determination. I see it in the deep furrows in their brow. I feel it in the tightness of the muscles in their hands. I respect that kind of human strength. But the distinguishing mark of people whose strength comes from God is that they hold on with joy and thanksgiving. I see it in the peaceful expression in their eyes. I feel it in the warm clasp of their hands. Within their strong endurance, I have seen a hopeful realization of God's steadfast love and an over-flowing sense of gratitude for every sign of God's goodness in their lives. Instead of hardship making them bitter, it makes them better. Instead of grim determination, they endure their suffering with grate-ful dependence upon God.

In his final bequest to Solomon, David commissioned his son for the task ahead. We need to pass on the same kind of commission to our children. "Now set your mind and heart to seek the LORD your God. Go and build the sanctuary of the LORD God" (1 Chronicles 22:19).

Jesus' version of that challenge to "set your mind and heart to seek the Lord" is recorded in the Sermon on the Mount (Matthew 5:1–7:29). He said we cannot serve multiple masters. We cannot live fully effective lives with divided loyalties. We cannot serve both God and anything else. I remember as a kid at summer camp hearing our youth leaders offer the ultimatum "Either Christ is Lord of all, or he is not Lord at all." Jesus called his disciples to "seek first the Kingdom—the rule, the reign, the purpose—of God, along with God's right-relatedness, and then everything else will fall into its proper place" (Matthew 6:33, paraphrased).

What does it mean to "set your mind and your heart to seek the Lord"? I think it means focusing the central part of my being, the con-trol center of my personality, the central core of my life on God's pur-pose and will revealed in Jesus, so that the Spirit of God can give order and meaning to everything else from the inside out. This is what Paul was describing when he challenged us:

If you have been raised with Christ, seek the things that are above, where Christ is, seated at the right hand of God. Set your minds on things that are above, not on things that are on earth, for you have died, and your life is hidden with Christ in God. (Colossians 3:1-3)

Paul got downright specific about what that mindset looks like. He told the Colossian Christians to put to death things like "fornication, impurity, passion, evil desire, . . . greed (which is [a form of] idolatry). . . . . anger, wrath, malice, slander, and abusive language. . . . Do not lie" (Colossians 3:5-9). In contrast, a mindset that is focused on the risen Christ results in "compassion, kindness, humility, meekness, and patience" as well as forgiveness, and "love, which binds everything together in perfect harmony" (Colossians 3:12-14).

Every day, in the ordinary activities of life, we choose either to set our lives in the direction of God's will revealed in Jesus or to set our lives in the direction of our own self-will and self-oriented desires. Day in and day out, we have the power to choose the things that will hold our attention, inform our decisions, and determine our behavior. Both the challenge and the opportunity of the spiritual life is to set our minds on things that are above; to seek, above all else, the rule and reign of God; to set our minds and hearts to seek the Lord.

Richard Rohr's study of the rites of passage for boys into manhood led him to the conclusion that "you can only give away what you have. If the fathers have not gone through significant spiritual passages themselves, they really have nothing to say to young men" (*Sojourners*, May–June 1998; p. 19). The disturbing reality about your life and mine is that we can't give away what we don't have. We can only pass on to our children the spiritual values and faith we have found for ourselves. The only way to prepare a valuable spiritual estate for our heirs is to nurture within ourselves the kind of spiritual life we would like to pass on to them.

Morrie Schwartz was a professor at Brandeis University. While dying with Lou Gehrig's disease, he passed on his most important lessons to his student Mitch Albom. Albom passed them on to the rest of us in the runaway bestseller *Tuesdays with Morrie*. Reading it is like listening to David pass on the lessons of his life to Solomon. The response to Albom's book I've been hearing from all kinds of men confirms our deep desire to receive the gifts of life experience from spiritual mentors and fathers-in-the-faith.

"Mitch," he said, "the culture doesn't encourage you to think about such things until you're about to die. We're so wrapped up with egotistical things, career, family, having enough money, meeting the mortgage, getting a new car, fixing the radiator when it breaks—we're involved in trillions of little acts just to keep going. So we don't get into the habit of standing back and looking at our lives and saying, Is this all? Is this all I want? Is something missing?"

"Everyone knows they're going to die," he said again, "but nobody believes it. If we did, we would do things differently."

"The truth is, Mitch," he said, "Once you learn how to die, you learn how to live."

(*Tuesdays With Morrie*, New York: Doubleday, 1997, pp. 64-65, 81-82)

The best thing we can leave the kids is a living model of what it means to live by faith, to live from the inside out, and to die in peace.

I will sing of your steadfast love, O LORD, forever;
    with my mouth I will proclaim your faithfulness to all generations.
I declare that your steadfast love is established forever;
    your faithfulness is as firm as the heavens.

You said, "I have made a covenant with my chosen one,
    I have sworn to my servant David:
'I will establish your descendants forever,
    and build your throne for all generations.' "
. . . .
Forever I will keep my steadfast love for him,
    and my covenant with him will stand firm.
. . . .
If his children forsake my law
    and do not walk according to my ordinances,
if they violate my statutes
    and do not keep my commandments,
then I will punish their transgression with the rod
    and their iniquity with scourges;
but I will not remove from him my steadfast love,
    or be false to my faithfulness.
. . . .
Who can live and never see death?
    Who can escape the power of Sheol?
. . . .
Blessed be the LORD forever. Amen and Amen.
                          (Psalm 89:1-4, 28, 30-33, 48, 52)

Time Out

F
A
T
H
E
R
I
N
G

1. *Prepare your estate.* What would you like to leave the kids? Make a list of the specific personal and spiritual values you would like to pass on to the next generation.

2. *Evaluate your spiritual legacy.* Look closely at the inheritance David passed on to Solomon:
   • Calling: "My life is not about me."
   • Peacemaking: "He shall be a man of peace."
   • Wisdom: "Understanding what to do with what we learn."
   • Strength and good courage: "Enduring with joy."
   • Commission: "Set your mind on the Lord."

   How are you doing at passing these bequests on to your children? How can you see these gifts at work in your life?

3. *Learn to live.* Reread the words from Morrie Schwartz. (If you have not read the entire book, you may wish to purchase it on your next trip to the bookstore.) What would you do differently if you knew you were going to die? (After all, you know that already!) How does learning to die teach you how to live?

4. *Prayer.* John and Charles Wesley lived in a day when death was an ever-present reality. Limited medical care, the unsanitary squalor of the slums of London, and the oppressive effects of poverty could all result in a sudden and painful demise. Charles Wesley knew that he was touching on a deep fear within the lives of his people when he wrote:

FATHERING

And am I born to die?
    To lay this body down?
And must my trembling spirit fly
    Into a world unknown?
    A land of deepest shade,
    Unpierced by human thought!
The dreary regions of the dead,
    Where all things are forgot!
. . . .

O thou, that wouldst not have
    One wretched sinner die,
Who diedst thyself my soul to save
    From endless misery!
    Show me the way to shun
    Thy dreadful wrath severe,
That, when thou comest on thy throne,
    I may with joy appear!

Thou art thyself the Way;
    Thyself in me reveal;
So shall I spend my life's short day
    Obedient to thy will;
    So shall I love my God,
    Because he first loved me,
And praise thee in thy bright abode
    To all eternity.

                              Charles Wesley

Endings

A Song for the Last Inning

1 Chronicles 29

Our future, however far we look, is the natural extension of the faith by which we live now and the life in which we now participate. Eternity is now in flight and we with it.

—*Dallas Willard,* The Divine Conspiracy

I watch a lot of people die. I've been there with older adults who died at peace, with parents who watched in horror as their teenagers' mangled bodies were taken from a crushed car, with midcareer people who died too soon, and with parents who carried their daughter's body in their arms to the hospital for cremation. Being there at the end of human existence is a sacred privilege of pastoral ministry.

I still remember the first parishioner I watched die with cancer. I was a spiffy new associate pastor, fresh out of seminary and green as grass after a summer rain. I graduated from seminary before Elisabeth Kübler-Ross taught us the stages of dying, before "clinical pastoral education" in hospital settings became a basic staple for ministerial training, and before *hospice* became a household word for terminally ill patients. Having graduated from a very reputable seminary, I have every confidence that we discussed ministry with terminally ill patients in a course on pastoral care. But whatever I learned in that classroom quickly evaporated in my first week on the job when my senior pastor said, "Come on, Jim, there's someone you need to meet. He wants to check out the new pastor."

The man we went to visit was a longtime member of the congregation, one of those all-around good guys whose life was a model of healthy faith, vibrant friendships, and manly love. Instead of preparing to retire from his business, he was preparing to die. He was facing cancer in one of its most miserable, debilitating, painful forms. He had been through the surgery, the radiation, the endless hours of treatment, and now he had been taken home to die. His master bedroom had become a temporary medical center. I remember the tubes, the bandages, and the smell. I remember the violent hiccups that shook the bed and drained him of all his strength. I never knew that hiccups could be so cruel! But most of all, I remember the sparkle in his eye, the warmth of his spirit, and the surprising strength in his grip as he shook the hand of his new pastor and welcomed me into the final days of his life. At this parishioner's funeral a few weeks later, the senior pastor demonstrated uncharacteristic emotion when his voice cracked as he spoke. He said that we represented all the pastors who had served that church and had been blessed by this man's support and friendship.

There began a long line of faithful people who have allowed me to be with them on the sacred journey toward the ending of their lives. They've been some of my best teachers, and here is one of the most important lessons I've learned. People generally die the way they live. There aren't a lot of surprises about the way folks come to the ending of their lives. They usually face death the same way they have faced life. If they were grouchy, self-centered, pain-in-the-butt folks when they were at full strength, I don't expect them to become the nicest folks in town when they are dying. But if they have lived with grace, patience, faith, and joy, that's generally the way they die.

My observation is that men who live from the "outside in" tend to face death in a cold, clinical way. Having kept soul-level realities at a distance throughout their lives, they continue to deny their deepest feelings, hurts, hopes and fears as they approach death. By contrast, men who live from the "inside out," those who have developed the spiritual disciplines by which the word, will, and way of Jesus Christ become a living reality within the depths of their beings, come to the end of their human stories with soul-strengthening resources of inner peace, genuine gratitude, and confident hope. Just the way a runner brings to the last mile of the marathon the physical strength that has been developed through long hours of disciplined training, we bring to the ending of life the spiritual resources we have nurtured along the way, no more and no less.

We might as well face it: we all will die. Death is the most universally democratic experience of human existence; none of us is going to get out of here alive! The question is not *whether* we die, but *how* we die, which is directly related to how we live and the spiritual resources we have developed along the way. So, what can we learn from being there at the end of David's story?

I cannot look at the Bible's final pictures of David without thinking of Winston Churchill, whose presence influenced the history of Great Britain the way David's life shaped the history of Israel. When Hugh Brogan reviewed Martin Gilbert's 1,066 page biography of Churchill for *The New York Times*, he said, "The supreme duty of every biographer of Winston Churchill is to be enthralled, since the story that has to be told is so full of historical drama and rich humanity." Brogan summed up the life of Britain's greatest prime minister by saying, "Almost everything he ever wrote or said was touched with inimitable life" (*The New York Times Book Review*, December 8, 1991; p. 18).

In a similar way, I am enthralled with David's story. His life was so full of historical drama. Indeed, the historical impact of his reign continues to influence the politics of the Middle East today. As a political/military/national leader, David is hard to beat. And yet, the most enthralling thing about him is his rich humanity. David is no plaster saint; this guy is for real.

From the moment David steps onto the stage as an adolescent shepherd, he not only captures our attention; he takes our hearts. We find healing in his songs and courage in his sling. We struggle with him in his conflict with Saul, and we rejoice with him in his friendship with Jonathan. We celebrate his victories and share the disappointment in his defeats. We dance with him before the altar of God, and we stumble with him in his lust for sexual prowess and political power. We sing his psalms of praise for the faithfulness of God, and we weep over the deadly consequences of his arrogance and sin. Like watching the final act of Shakespeare's *King Lear,* we wind our way through the tangled confusion of David's final days with more compassion than outrage. After the near collapse of the kingdom during Absalom's rebellion, we sigh with relief when Solomon prepares to reign. In the triumph and tragedy of David's story we can see both our human struggles and the relentless purpose of God being worked out in often inscrutable ways. Through it all, the God of steadfast love (*hesed*) has been faithful to the divine purpose for which David was called. The king comes to the ending of life with the vision of the future still before his eyes, "in a good old age, full of days, riches, and honor" (1 Chronicles 29:28). In the rich humanity of his strength and weakness, success and failure, obedience and sin, we feel the rhythm of inimitable life; life that is full of passion, infused with power, and reverberating with praise.

Being there with David at the ending of his story can teach us to live with passion. By "passion" I do not mean the self-centered lust cele-brated by the bumper sticker on a truck that is parked down the street from my house. It declares, "Trust Your Lust." David tried that! Giving way to his lust for sex and power was the cause of his greatest troubles. The ironic twist in David's story—some would say it is an expression of divine justice or a Hebrew sense of humor—is that the king whose story turns on a moment of self-satisfying, promiscuous, sexual lust comes to the end of his life impotent and cold, unaroused by the beau-tiful young servant girl who is chosen to keep him warm (1 Kings 1:1-4). It just goes to prove that you really *can't* trust your lust!

Spiritual passion comes from a deeper place than lust. It's what Sam Keen called "a fire in the belly." Keen got that image from Jeremiah, the Old Testament prophet who described the presence of God in his life as "a burning fire shut up in my bones" (Jeremiah 20:9). Like the fire that Moses saw in the bush that burned but was not consumed, the fire of God's presence in Jeremiah's bones could not be quenched. The nineteenth-century poet George Croly described the same spiritual passion when he prayed

> Teach me to love thee as thine angels love,
> one holy passion filling all my frame;
> the kindling of the heaven-descended Dove,
> my heart an altar, and thy love the flame.
> (from "Spirit of God, Descend on My Heart")

In David's farewell address to the leaders of the kingdom, he remembers the day that "holy passion" was ignited in his heart: "The LORD God of Israel chose me . . . [and] took delight in making me king over all Israel" (1 Chronicles 28:4). Looking back across the years at the way God continued to be faithful to that calling, David could promise Solomon that the Lord "will not fail you or forsake you, until all the work for the service of the house of the LORD is finished"

(1 Chronicles 28:20). The passion within David's bones was the deep sense of God's purpose being fulfilled in his life. It was a fire that burned from the inside out of his life. David's final act as king was to lead the people in offering their sacrifices in thanksgiving to God, "and they ate and drank before the LORD on that day with great joy" (1 Chronicles 29:22).

Keen says that one of the garden-variety effects of stress among men today is that we "rustout" rather than "burnout." It is the product, he says, "not of an excess of fire but of a deficiency of passion" (*Fire in the Belly*, New York: Bantam, 1991, p. 61). I've seen people "rustout." They end up weary, bored, empty, and simply wearing down to the end. I felt it from a fellow pastor who said with a deep sigh, "Well, just twenty more months until retirement." There was no excess of fire that would burn him out; just a joyless boredom that was eating away at his soul. But I've also seen people for whom the fire of life, the warmth of love, the flame of hope, the spark of a vision of the future burned like a passion within them to the last moment of their human existence. Like David, they came to the end of their lives with great gratitude and joy.

Admiral Joe Fowler was one of those folks with a passion in his bones. He led the Pacific fleet during World War II and could have gone to the Pentagon at the end of the war. Instead, he retired from the Navy and went to work with a dreamer named Walt Disney. He caught the vision and went to work to buy up the Florida orange groves and swampland that would one day become Walt Disney World. Joe Fowler supervised every detail of the construction of the Magic Kingdom. When I got to know him, he was in his eighties and the Disney folks had just called him back to consult on another project. He was still thinking, growing, and dreaming of the future. As his body weakened, the fire within him continued to burn. He was ninety-nine years old when he died, "in a good old age, full of days" (1 Chronicles 29:28). I still hear his New England accent as he called out, "Cheerio!"

I'd like to come to the ending of life with that kind of passion. I'd like to end this story with the fire of God's love still burning in my bones; with deep gratitude for the amazing faithfulness of God; with an abiding sense of joy in the goodness of life.

Being there with David at the ending of his story can also teach us to live with power. Not power of the kind that David grasped for on the outside, but the inner power that grows out of a deep assurance that the God who has been with us throughout our lives will continue to be with us in death. David expresses that kind of inner power when he challenges Solomon to "be strong and of good courage. . . . For the LORD God, my God, is with you" (1 Chronicles 28:20).

Don't miss the personal connection in David's words: "The Lord God, *my* God, is with you." The God who took possession of an unknown shepherd boy and was relentlessly faithful to the divine purpose for his life is now the God whom David claims as his own. God is not some vague, abstract power, a distant deity who looks down from heaven in judgment. Through the long journey of David's life, God has become an intimate presence, like an old friend upon whom David can fully and ultimately depend. When every form of human power is being stripped away, David is held in the grip of a profoundly personal sense of the power of God.

When it comes down to it, I have a very pragmatic reason for practicing the spiritual disciplines that nurture a growing, healthy relationship with God. I do it during my life because I don't want to be alone at the end. When the career is over, when the kids are grown, when the weakness of an aging body robs me of physical strength and sexual prowess, when all the things that shape life from the outside in become powerless, I want to be left with a powerful relationship with God. I want to know that the God who claimed me as his own child in my baptism has become "my God" in a way that brings wholeness, peace, and hope to the deepest places in my soul.

I receive a bundle of church newsletters in the mail each week; I always read the one that comes from First United Methodist Church in Ormond Beach, Florida, where Phil Roughton has a way of saying what I wish I had said. He recently wrote:

> A long time ago, I noticed [that] religion either makes people really healthy—or really sick. About the same time, I decided I wanted to be part of the former, not the latter! You might see it differently (!), but I believe God is faithfully teaching me how to do that, and providing all the grace required to make it possible. And I underline that word "grace." Religion, for many, is nothing more than a system for staying in control. Grace-driven *relationship* with God through Jesus has the power to restore you to God's original, liberated, joy-filled, peace-characterized design. Though we make the choice to participate, it is God's work. And it's a gift of love.

This was Phil's way of describing his growing relationship with God, the kind of healthy, grace-filled relationship that can release the power of God in our lives.

Across the years I've discovered that the person who has nurtured this kind of relationship with God can continue to believe in God's vision even if that person does not live to see it fulfilled. While serving the church in Orlando, Florida, I was a member of a group of people who were committed to learning Jesus' way of nonviolence and peace. One woman in the group had been a part of the Christian community that was active in the nonviolent peace and civil rights movements in the 1960s. She shared a prayer that was a part of the daily liturgy of that community and had become a consistent part of her spiritual life. The prayer asked for "a tenacity which will not let go until the final battle closes, and a nonchalance that the final battle's closing does not depend on our existence."

Knowing the power of God within our souls means that we do not need to see all the victories in our own lifetimes. We don't need to see all the swords turned into plowshares and all the spears turned into pruning hooks. We don't need to see every problem solved, every sickness healed, every pain comforted. In the end, it will be enough to know that we discovered what it means to be a part of God's redeeming purpose in human history. It will be enough to have tenaciously held on to the promise that one day God's kingdom will come and God's will shall be done on earth as it is already done in heaven. It will be enough to know that God has somehow used our lives, actions, choices, and decisions as a witness to God's relentless purpose of redeeming love for the whole world. We can have a faithful nonchalance because we know that the final victory does not depend on our existence. David came to the end of his life with that kind of relationship with God, and I'd like to come to the ending with it, too.

Being there with David at the ending of his story can also teach us to live with praise. In the Bible's last snapshot of David, we find the king whose story began with the songs he sang for Saul praising God in worship:

> Then David blessed the LORD in the presence of all the assembly; David said: "Blessed are you, O LORD, the God of our ancestor Israel, forever and ever. Yours, O LORD, are the greatness, the power, the glory, the victory, and the majesty; for all that is in the heavens and on

the earth is yours; yours is the kingdom, O Lord, and you are exalted as head above all. . . . And now, our God, we give thanks to you and praise your glorious name. . . . For all things come from you, and of your own have we given you. For we are aliens and transients before you." (1 Chronicles 29:10-15)

I worshiped at the Riverside Church in New York City on the Sunday following Nelson Rockefeller's funeral. Rockefeller's grandfather had funded the building, which towers over Riverside Drive. It was a powerful setting in which to hear the Reverend William Sloan Coffin remind us, "All of us are transients on this earth, even the Rockefellers." Ultimately we do not "own" anything; everything we have and are is a gift from God, the One who holds the title deed to the whole creation. To live with praise is to live with a deep awareness of the One from whom all good things come.

Tim Crews was the "all-American boy": good-looking, athletic, optimistic, with a day-brightening smile that lit up the room when he walked in. He had a contagious laugh, the kind of laughter that is born out of an energetic love of life. I remember the first time Tim and Laurie came to see me, two college kids who wanted to get married. I keep a picture of their wedding in my file. I remember the day I baptized Tim and received Tim and Laurie into the church.

Baseball was Tim's passion. He went to college on an athletic scholarship with one goal in mind: to be a Major League pitcher. He had been groomed for it since the first time he picked up a ball in Little League. I remember the day Tim finally made it to "the show" as a relief pitcher for the Dodgers. He was on the team when they won the World Series in 1988. I remember the day he came home with a ring, a smile, and a great future before him. And I remember the day, four years later, when I turned on the early morning news and heard that he had been killed in a boating accident, leaving his wife and the three children I had baptized.

Orel Hershiser, the pitcher who led the Dodgers to the World Series, was at the funeral. Before the service we laughed together about a story Tim loved to tell. It was the eighth inning of the final game of the Series. Hershiser was on the mound, but he was having a tough time. The fans, who usually supported him, were on his back. Suddenly, Hershiser stopped. He stepped back from the mound, looked up to the sky, and paused in silence for what felt like a long time. Then he stepped back onto the mound to pitch the rest of the inning and went on to win the game.

In the locker room a reporter asked him, "What were you doing out there in the bottom of the eighth?" Hershiser surprised the reporter by saying he was singing a hymn. When Hershiser was a guest on *The Tonight Show,* Johnny Carson asked the question every baseball-watching preacher in the country wanted to ask, "What was the hymn?" Right there, on national late-night television, Hershiser began to sing what traditional churchgoers know as the "Doxology":

> Praise God, from whom all blessings flow;
> Praise him, all creatures here below;
> Praise him above, ye heavenly host;
> Praise Father, Son, and Holy Ghost.

Carson was speechless. It was one of those unique moments when he simply didn't know what to say. There may even have been a tear in his eye.

After Tim told me that story, I used it for a sermon entitled "A Song for the Eighth Inning." In preparation for his funeral I pulled that sermon from the file again and lifted this paragraph from it.

> When the pressure is on; when everything seems to be stacked up against you; when the hostile world tries to beat you down and the very things that used to be a source of encouragement become a burden; when you're tired and weary and you wonder if you have the strength to go on; when it seems as if the goal toward which you are moving is beyond your reach; when you're in the bottom of the eighth inning, do you have the kind of inner faith, nurtured by a consistent way of living and being with Christ, that will give you the strength to hang in there so you can go out and pitch again?

Facing the devastating reality of Tim's death, I added, "God help us, we're in the bottom of the eighth inning. It leaves us speechless and in pain. But even as we face the dark power of death, we can praise God for the gift of life and for the assurance of God's love that will never let us go." I paraphrased the Doxology to say:

Praise God, from whom the blessing of this life flows;
Praise God, all of us here below who are in tears;
Praise God, the heavenly hosts, which we dare to
believe that Tim has joined;
Praise Father, Son, and Holy Ghost. Amen.

David comes to the last inning of his life with the Doxology on his lips.
He faces the ending of life with a profound awareness of the greatness
and goodness of God. He praises the God who claimed him in his
childhood and never let him go. Looking back across his life, David
cannot help declaring, "This God—his way is perfect; / the promise of
the LORD proves true" (2 Samuel 22:31). We hear this same declaration also in Eugene Peterson's paraphrase of David's words in Psalm
18:18-24:

God stuck by me.
He stood me up on a wide-open field;
    I stood there saved—surprised to be loved!

God made my life complete
    when I placed all the pieces before him.
When I got my act together,
    he gave me a fresh start.
Now I'm alert to God's ways;
    I don't take God for granted.
Every day I review the ways he works;
    I try not to miss a trick.
I feel put back together,
    and I'm watching my step.
God rewrote the text of my life
    when I opened the book of my heart to his eyes.
                    (Psalm 18:18-24 *The Message*)

For the biblical writers, the big story is not what David did but what
God did through him. From beginning to end, God is the main character in this drama. Through all the very human stuff of David's
strength and weakness, victory and defeat, God was faithful to the
promise he made the day Samuel poured the anointing oil on his head.
   It was hard not to love the late composer and conductor Leonard
Bernstein: all that passion, all that energy, all that hair flying in every

direction when he directed. When you watched him conduct the New York Philharmonic, you sensed that the music started somewhere down in his toes, surged through every molecule of his being, and flowed from him into the orchestra. There was a hunger and a thirst within him that *had* to be fulfilled in music. The morning after his death, the *Today* show ran a taped interview with Bernstein, in which he said:

> I'm hearing the ideal performance of the score I've been buried with night and day, and I'm making this constant comparison between the ideal and what I'm hearing. When there is no difference, I'm in heaven.

To live by faith is to know that in Jesus Christ we have heard, felt, and seen the ideal performance of human life. To live from the inside out is to constantly compare that ideal performance with what we experience of reality, and to hunger and thirst for there to be no difference; to live with hope is to know that in heaven, the two will be one.

I was there when Waller McCleskey died at the age of eighty-two. He was a faithful layman whose spiritual and genetic roots sank deep into the soil of Methodism in Georgia. From the outside in, he had been weakened by over a decade of medical treatment for various physical problems. But from the inside out, he was filled with inimitable life. It was born out of the love of Christ, empowered by a faithful relationship with God, and expressed in constant praise for the good gifts of God. We began his memorial service with Charles Wesley's grand anthem of Methodism, "O For a Thousand Tongues to Sing." The final phrase of the hymn caught my attention as it never had before:

> Anticipate your heaven below,
> And own that love is heaven.

For Waller, as for Wesley, "anticipate your heaven below" did not mean sitting around daydreaming about floating off into the sky someday. "Anticipate your heaven below" means living in the present on the basis of what we believe about the future. It means living here on earth in ways that are consistent with the way we expect to live in heaven. Waller taught me that to "anticipate your heaven below" means filling every moment with all the life and love it can contain. It means living in overflowing gratitude for every good gift that comes our way. It means squeezing every ounce of love and life out of every human experience. It means living so fully and freely in the love of God that this life on earth becomes a finite, human expression of the infinite life of heaven. To "*own* that love is heaven" means that the steadfast love of God is constantly within our grasp. Through our experience of the love of God on earth, we experience the infinite love that is fulfilled in heaven.

At the end of his life, Waller said it best. Less than an hour before he passed through death to life eternal, he asked Doris, "How much longer do I have?" They had been married for fifty-nine years. They knew that their vow to be faithful to each other "until death us do part" would not keep them together much longer. She replied, "Only the Lord knows that." Waller leaned back on his pillow, looked her in the eye, smiled, and said, "It's been a great life!" At the conclusion of his funeral, we led his casket from the sanctuary with the pipe organ echoing the Doxology behind us.

What a way to come to the last inning of life! What a way for the story to end! What a way to live! And what a way to "own that love is heaven."

Time Out

E
N
D
I
N
G
S

Spirituality is a life-and-death deal. The way we live is the way we die. John Wesley caught the urgency of spiritual discipline when he challenged the early Methodists:

> Spare no pains to preserve always a deep, a continual, a lively, and a joyful sense of [God's] gracious presence. Cheerfully, expect that He before whom you stand will ever guide you with his eye, will support you by his guardian hand, will keep you from all evil, and "when you have suffered a while, will make you perfect, will stablish, strengthen, and settle you," and then "preserve you unblamable unto the coming of our Lord Jesus Christ." (Sermon 111, "On the Omnipresence of God")

1. *Being there at death.* What is your experience with death? What have you learned from people whom you have "watched" die (regardless of whether you were physically present at the end)? Do you agree that "people generally die the way they live"?

2. *Being there through life.* Look back across David's story. What are the most important lessons you have learned? How have you been enthralled by his story? What are the most important spiritual lessons you have learned in your life?

3. *Living with passion.* What really turns you on? How have you experienced the difference between "burnout" and "rustout"? How have you known or seen the kind of spiritual passion that burned within Jeremiah's bones (Jeremiah 20:9)?

4. *Living with power.* What does it mean for you to say "*my* God"? What spiritual disciplines have you dis-

E N D I N G S

covered in David's story that can help you develop the personal relationship with God that David described? What practical steps will you take to maintain that relationship?

5. *Living with praise.* What difference does it make for you to know that we are all temporary residents here and that God holds the title deed to the creation? Orel Hershiser turned to the words of the Doxology at a time when he felt he needed to call upon their strength; describe a time in your life when you called upon the power and praise of God to provide the strength you needed. Read Eugene Peterson's paraphrase of Psalm 18 again. Where can you find yourself in David's words?

6. *Living forever.* What does "heaven" mean to you? How are you anticipating heaven below—right here on earth, right now?

7. *Prayer:*
   Spirit of God, descend upon my heart;
   wean it from earth; through all its pulses move;
   stoop to my weakness, mighty as thou art,
   and make me love thee as I ought to love.

   I ask no dream, no prophet ecstasies,
   no sudden rending of the veil of clay,
   no angel visitant, no opening skies;
   but take the dimness of my soul away.

   Hast thou not bid me love thee, God and King?
   All, all thine own, soul, heart and strength and mind.
   I see thy cross; there teach my heart to cling.
   O let me seek thee, and O let me find!

   Teach me to feel that thou art always nigh;
   teach me the struggles of the soul to bear.

E
N
D
I
N
G
S

To check the rising doubt, the rebel sigh,
teach me the patience of unanswered prayer.

Teach me to love thee as thine angels love,
one holy passion filling all my frame;
the kindling of the heaven-descended Dove,
my heart an altar, and thy love the flame.

George Croly